D0791954

Paws to Consider

Brian Kilcommons and Sarah Wilson

Paws

Choosing the Right Dog for You and Your Family

to Consider

WARNER BOOKS

A Time Warner Company

Warner Books, Inc., 1271 Avenue of the Americas,
New York, NY 10020
Visit our Web site at www.warnerbooks.com

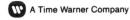 A Time Warner Company

Printed in the United States of America
First Warner Books Printing: September 1999
10 9 8 7 6 5 4 3 2 1

Library of Congress Cataloging-in-Publication Data

Kilcommons, Brian.
    Paws to consider : choosing the right dog for you and
your family / Brian Kilcommons and Sarah Wilson.
        p.   cm.
    Includes index.
    ISBN 0-446-52151-5
    1. Dogs.   2. Dogs—Selection.   3. Dog breeds.
I. Wilson, Sarah, 1960–   . II. Title.
SF426.K524   1999
636.7'088'7—dc21   98-32300
                                                        CIP

BOOK DESIGN BY RALPH L. FOWLER

In loving memory of

Dorothy Johnson,

whose insight, honesty, and loyalty are deeply missed. She was a quiet crusader for humane care of all animals, a fact that every dog she met seemed to know.

Acknowledgments

To all our clients through the years who have helped us understand these breeds better.

Many of the following people helped us, either in the present or the past, in person or through their writing, to understand this subject more completely.

Others gave generously of their time, as honest sounding boards and brilliant, insightful readers. By necessity, this is only a partial listing. You know who you are:

Doug Antuna, Dr. Louis Berman, Marsha Blodgett, Eric and Gemi Brickson, Graham Buck, Roger and Jill Caras, Beth Chaney, Gwenn Chaney, Glenn Ciottone, Michael Clemens, Suzanne Clothier, Chet Collier, Tammy Conmay, Sandy Cornwell, Vicki Croke, Elizabeth Dunn, Mrs. Muriel Freeman, Marilyn and Peter Gates, Marge Gibbs, Dr. John Greenfield, Barbara Hearst, Dr. John Higgins, Dianne Hopper, Ninon Hutchinson, Helen and Charlie Ingher, Toni Kay, Suzanne Kinder, Diane Laratta, Ann Lithgo, Mary Mandich, Dr. Jim McKeirnan,

KELLY ROGERS

Shirley Minatelli, Dr. Mike Moyer, Lily Mummert, Beth Ostrander, Dr. George Padgett, Christine Pellicano, CJ Puotinen, John Rogerson, Linda Rose, Louise Schofield, Marc Street, Mary Ann and Tony Svizeny, Mrs. Joseph Thomas, Walter and Jane Turken, Suzannah Valentinetti, Joan Webb, Barbara Woodhouse, Dr. Michelle Yasson, Dr. Lawrence Zola.

Contents

Introduction   1

So You Want a Dog   3

Why Do You Want a Dog?   4
What a Dog Will Demand   6
When Is the Best Time to Get a Dog?   10
Which One for Me?   12

How to Find Your Friend   15

Researching a Breed   15
  Resources   15
    Books   15
    Magazines   16
    The Internet   16
    Videos   16
    Veterinarians, Trainers, Groomers   17
    Rescue Groups   17
The Finalists   18
Crib Notes on Genetic Disease   22
Finding a Breeder   26
Rescue Groups   28
Shelters   29
Pet Stores   29
Making Your Choice   30
Choosing an Adult Dog   33

Your Dog – Then and Now   35

Terriers   35
Retrievers   37

SARAH WILSON

Spaniels   39
Pointers   40
Setters   41
Flock Guards   42
Scent Hounds   43
Sighthounds   45
Property Guards   46
Draft/Rescue Dogs   49
Sled Dogs   50
Toys   51
Herding Dogs   53
Non-Sporting/Rare   54

BOB & KAREN ARENDS

Understanding the Breed Chapters   57

Good Dogs That Are Hard to Find   63

American Cocker Spaniel   64
Beagle   66
Doberman Pinscher   68
English Springer Spaniel   70
German Shepherd Dog   72
Golden Retriever   74
Great Dane   76
Labrador Retriever   78
Toy and Miniature Poodles   80

The Nine-to-Five Dog   83

Borzoi   84
English Cocker Spaniel   86
French Bulldog   88
Greyhound   90
Irish Wolfhound   92
Pekingese   94

SARAH WILSON

Pug   96
Shih Tzu   98
Whippet   100

The Family Dog   103

Bernese Mountain Dog   104
Cavalier King Charles Spaniel   106
Collie   108
English Setter   110
Keeshond   112
Newfoundland   114
Samoyed   116
Standard Poodle   118
Welsh Springer Spaniel   120

The High-Input, High-Output Dog   123

Alaskan Malamute   124
Bearded Collie   126
Belgian Sheepdog   128
Boxer   130
Brittany   132
Flat-Coated Retriever   134
German Shorthaired Pointer   136
Petit Basset Griffon Vendeen   138
Siberian Husky   140
Staffordshire Bull Terrier   142
Vizsla   144

The City Dog   147

Basset Hound   148
Boston Terrier   150
Bullmastiff   152
Cardigan Welsh Corgi   154

JOHN MINATELLI

DIANE LARATTA

Standard Dachshund   156
Norwich Terrier/Norfolk Terrier   158
Scottish Terrier   160
Shiba Inu   162
Tibetan Terrier   164
Welsh Terrier   166

The Indoor Companion   169

Chihuahua   172
Italian Greyhound   174
Japanese Chin   176
Maltese   178
Miniature Dachshund   180
Papillon   182
Yorkshire Terrier   184

The Low-Shed Breeds   187

Airedale   188
Australian Terrier   190
Bichon Frise   192
Bouvier des Flandres   194
Cairn Terrier   196
Chinese Crested   198
Miniature Schnauzer   200
Portuguese Water Dog   202
Soft-Coated Wheaten Terrier   204
Standard Schnauzer   206
West Highland White Terrier   208

The Watchdog   211

Chesapeake Bay Retriever   212
Great Pyrenees   214
Miniature Pinscher   216

Norwegian Elkhound   218
Pembroke Welsh Corgi   220
Pomeranian   222
Rhodesian Ridgeback   224
Schipperke   226
Shetland Sheepdog   228
Silky Terrier   230

Not for Everyone   233

Akita   234
American Pit Bull Terrier   235
Australian Shepherd   235
Basenji   236
Border Collie   236
Bloodhound   236
Bulldog   237
Chinese Shar Pei   237
Chow Chow   238
Dalmatian   238
Jack Russell Terrier   239
Irish Setter   239
Lhasa Apso   240
Old English Sheepdog   240
Rottweiler   240
Saint Bernard   241
Weimaraner   241

Resources   243
Index   247

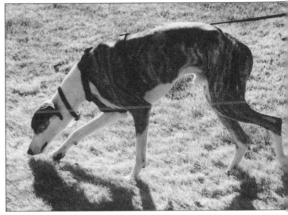

DIANE LARATTA

JILL ARNEL

Introduction

Perhaps we should not have written this book. If you all start making educated, sensible decisions, at least half of our business will fall away. What will we do without all the mismatches?

Mismatches like the intact male Rottweiler kept in a tiny third-floor apartment whose owners had to lean over the stairwell and listen for footsteps. If all was silent, they would hustle him downstairs. If they met someone coming up, they would retreat at a sprint to their apartment because the dog had claimed the entire building as his own.

What of the gorgeous Dalmatian owned by a busy working couple who had no time to exercise or train their picture-perfect dog? When she chewed their belongings and resisted their efforts to housebreak her, they called us. We told them over the phone that she needed more of their time, more free running in safe areas, and more behavioral direction, but they wanted to pay to hear the same advice in their apartment. Okay. We can do that.

DIANE LARATTA

God bless each too-cute-for-words Jack Russell Terrier puppy, because they grow up into feisty, strong-minded, brilliant adults. Obedience does not come swiftly. After all, they already know how they want to live their lives — why do they need our input?

What would we do without the endless, rainbow parade of Labradors? Purchased as the ideal, easy, family dog by trendy young couples everywhere, Labs are also oral, full-contact, exuberant animals who will drag you down the street to greet a stranger. Organizing them isn't difficult, but most people need some guidance.

If we really wanted to help our business, we could have filled this book with stunningly bad information, like Malamutes don't shed and Whippets love the cold. But we didn't. You deserve to know absolute truth about the dogs, and the dogs deserve to be known. "Absolute truth" is a relative term, but we've tried to be helpful based on our experience. If our business drops off a bit because of it, nothing would please us more!

With some information, finding the right breed isn't difficult. Finding the right dog is a pleasure. Having the companionship of such a dog is one of life's joys.

Know that somewhere, we are stroking a dog's head, or picking up a dog toy, or smiling as our dog romps with a stick—all things you will be enjoying soon.

So You Want a Dog

Right now, our five dogs mill around my chair lobbying for another walk out back. We've already gone on one hike down to the pond and another up the big hill, but it is getting late in the day and we all need to get out again.

These dogs demand daily training, supervision, and vigorous exercise to remain healthy and manageable. If we neglect our end of the bargain, if we are too busy or distracted to care for them properly, we will see our neglect in their restlessness.

If we were to neglect them for a few days, we might begin to see real tension in the group, more intensity over toys and food, bigger reactions toward strangers at the door. Keep up our neglect for a week and "bad" behaviors would bloom—maybe chewing, excessive barking, hyperactivity, or cat chasing. Those would be the dogs' behaviors, but they would be our fault.

Deciding to care for a dog is a serious decision. Dogs are dependent on you for their education, entertainment, health care, and safety. Canine care requires an investment of emotion, energy, cash, and time to do well, yet it is not worth doing any other way.

Why Do You Want a Dog?

The first thing to ask yourself is why you want a dog. Here are several of the most common reasons and what we think of them.

"FOR THE KIDS."

If you mean that by having a dog around, your children will learn empathy, caring, and unconditional love, then yes, "For the kids" is fine.

LARRY G. LOVIG

But if you mean that you're responding to constant pressure from your child on the provision that your child promises to do all the dog care (and what child has ever said, "Mom, you're right. I don't think I am mature enough for this large responsibility"?), then you are guaranteeing a bad experience for yourself, the dog, and, most important, your child.

Canine care is too big a venture for a child. Most adults find it challenging, especially for the first year or two. Children do not have mature levels of forethought, planning skills, or consistency. That's what makes them kids, besides being appreciably shorter than you. While caring for a family pet can certainly help build those qualities in your child, they are not normally present in a nine-year-old, nor should they be anticipated.

Expect to do nine-tenths of the work and to nag for the completion of the other tenth. If you become really good at training, you may be able to motivate your child to complete his or her dog-related chores without much reminding. If you manage to do that, write your own book and we'll buy it!

"FOR PROTECTION."

If you get a dog for this reason you are not alone, but you, and all the others who base this decision on fear, are setting yourself up for a fall. A dog is twenty-four hours a day, not just once or twice a year when you hear something go bump in the night. (A "something" more likely to be your cat jumping off the counter than Jack the Ripper entering your home.)

The large, powerful, assertive breeds that people choose when frightened are not the kinds of dogs that usually make easy, carefree pets. Nowadays it is not just your safety you have to worry about. Recently, an owner was convicted of murder for the death of a child mauled by her three large dogs. The tide is changing and the responsibility you have for your animal's behavior is increasing.

This is not only a tragedy for the people involved, it is a disaster for the dogs. Dogs selected and owned by people who are ill prepared for the responsibility are

Dog Owners Say Good-bye to

- Sleeping in on the weekend
- Food without hair
- A dry toilet seat
- Silk
- Leaving laundry on the floor
- Trash cans out in the open
- Going to dinner straight from work
- Spur of the moment getaways
- Dog-free friends

- White clothing
- Unbroken breakables
- Undisturbed rolls of toilet paper
- Sex in private
- Clean cars
- Stain-free carpets
- Walking barefoot
- Mud-free walls
- Dry tennis balls

making the ownership of all dogs increasingly difficult. Laws trying to legislate dog ownership are constantly on the docket. The favored tactic is to attempt to prohibit the ownership of any breed deemed dangerous, as if by eliminating a breed, you can eliminate the problem. We have news for those lawmakers: There are always other bigger and more assertive breeds than the ones that are popular now. The breed is not the problem; people's choices, and their management of those choices, are.

"TO BREED AND MAKE SOME MONEY."

Ha! By the time you breed, raise, train, care for, feed, groom, vaccinate, and buy equipment for your dogs, you will spend far more than you hoped to gain. We recently spoke to a woman who bred her Border Collie for extra cash. The bitch had trouble whelping, ending up with a cesarean. When the dog awoke, she wanted nothing to do with the pups. The owner was up around the clock trying to feed them. She had now spent hundreds of dollars on surgery, the puppies were dying, and the mother wasn't doing well.

With the millions of animals euthanized every year for lack of loving homes, leave the breeding to people who have studied their breed, done the necessary genetic testing, and carefully planned for the breeding. You can help your breed by neutering your pet(s).

"I WANT SOMETHING TO LOVE ME."

We all do, but that is not the reason to get a dog. A dog does not exist to fulfill your emotional needs, although she very well may help with some of them. Simply housing a dog so it's around when you need it is not enough. You need to teach, play, interact with, schedule your time around, tend to, understand, and love another being on its own terms—separate from you.

We have seen many dogs, especially toy breeds, spoiled to the point of neurosis by people who project all their own needs, fears, and worries onto those tiny shoulders. Give the dog a break!

"I WANT TO SHARE MY LIFE WITH AN ANIMAL."

Bingo! We have a winner. Your life will be changed. You are willing to invest whatever it takes to be a responsible caretaker. In the process, your children will learn empathy, you will feel safer and be unconditionally loved. What a great deal!

What a Dog Will Demand

Now that you have assessed your reason for getting a dog, let us consider what this decision will demand of your life.

ENERGY

Daily exercise will be some part of your life. If you choose one of the popular retriever breeds, exercise will be a *major* part of your life. Letting the dog out into the yard by himself does not count. You must actively interact with him to ensure that he gets the physical workout he requires.

SARAH WILSON

When the dog is young (under two years) he will need, above all, your attention and supervision. Get chatting on the phone and expect to clean up a mess of one kind or another. You'll be getting up earlier, staying active longer, and resting less. Those are not necessarily bad things, they are just factors to consider.

EMOTION

This is the immeasurable benefit and the infinite cost of becoming attached to a dog. Who would willingly give up a doggy smile first thing in the morning, the joyful blaze of intelligent recognition when the dog understands, the blessing of a dog's forgiveness, the gentleness of a quiet head resting on a knee? For many of us, and soon for you, too, life without at least one animal companion is unimaginable.

Balance this against unavoidable heartache. No beloved companion lives long enough. It is a great gift to be able to end suffering, yet it is a grave and terrible decision to make. To decide it is time to end the life of one of your best friends is always hard, even when you know it is right. Right and easy are different things; this is something you discover when you cradle your dog in your arms and love him out of this life the way he loved you in it.

EDUCATION

Mere possession of an animal or an object does not immediately endow you with expertise regarding it. We, for example, have owned and driven cars for several decades, and yet neither of us can rebuild a motor. Can you?

In this day and age, fewer and fewer of us are raised around animals. We live in a world that discovers animals more through television than through personal experience. For this and future generations, knowledge of animal behavior will have to be consciously acquired because it will not have had a chance to be previously absorbed.

BETH MARLEY

At a bare minimum, that means sitting in on a couple of local obedience classes, reading a few books, watching a few training videos. Our "Resources" section will refer you to some good sources.

Dog training is like cooking: There are many ways to do it and a lot of them are wonderful. Try not to get method-bound—the right method is the one that works for your dog and you, in this instance. The only common thread you'll find in "good" methods is that they are not abusive. Abuse is yelling, kicking, hanging, hitting, shaking, slapping, or in any way attacking the animal or unleashing your anger in the guise of education.

You're Driving Your Dog Crazy!

You will know you are out of control when you

- ➤ Cling to the bars of the cage, weeping uncontrollably, when your dog is left at a kennel.

- ➤ Sneak off from your husband every day on your honeymoon to call the kennel.

- ➤ Have your friends call the kennel daily to check up on the dog (they're calling from Italy).

- ➤ Buy your dog more outfits than you have.

- ➤ Feed your dog better than you feed yourself.

- ➤ Leave messages on the answering machine for your dog.

- ➤ Think the dog understands those messages.

Stay away from any trainer who recommends any of the above. While violence may cow a dog into submission in some instances (in others it will goad him into aggression), it will cost you a piece of the bond you two share.

Beyond that, whether you find a trainer who uses praise, play, or food as a motivator does not matter. You just want someone who motivates. Ideally, that motivation is combined with sensible, effective correction. A good correction is swift, to the point, used sparingly, and at a level that gets the desired results without creating new problems. If your dog stops jumping on people but now shies away, showing stress and fear, you haven't gained ground; you've lost it. Good corrections also work. If you have to use several in a row, stop. You are not being effective. That does not mean you have to correct harder, which is a common, but incorrect, assumption. If your timing is wrong, you aren't being clear, no foundation of understanding has been taught, or the dog is frightened, correcting harder is not the least bit educational.

Puppy class is always a good idea
SARAH WILSON

With good training, improvement happens swiftly. A dog who is taught with clarity and fun will be relaxed, with his tail wagging. Good trainers are not always easy to find, but they are well worth the effort to locate.

MONEY

Dogs cost money. Even if you adopt one for free, their spaying or neutering, yearly veterinary care, food, toys, and sundries add up. The larger the dog, the larger the bills. If you have a yard, for instance, you will need fencing.

Then there are the less expected expenses: the larger car when the dog simply does not fit in the hatchback, the air-conditioning because he gets so hot in the summer. Don't laugh too hard—we promise that you will make purchases for reasons you might not want to admit in open court. These can total a thousand dollars or more a year—easily over ten thousand dollars during the life of the dog. Are you ready for that financial commitment?

TIME

Most dogs require quite a bit of your time during the first few years. Depending on the temperament of the breed or mix you elect to live with, you may be looking at an hour or more a day for exercise, training, and/or grooming. Most breeds add time to

The Need to Be Needed

Dogs are social creatures. Humankind used that truth to mold the dog. The dog wanted us to want him and he still does. He is born with a desire to bond with us. The desire can be nurtured or ignored.

Do not get a dog if you plan to isolate him in the basement or outside. Separating a dog from "his" people on a regular and long-term basis is mental torture. Every cell in his body wants to be, and deserves to be, with you.

your housecleaning duties and some add a lot of time. Some breeds take less time but regardless of how calm your dog appears, he still needs your attention daily.

You can no longer go from work to a restaurant or out to a movie. A dog is a social animal who will become neurotic without your company. If you do not have this kind of time to give, choose a less demanding pet.

LIFESTYLE

If you live in an all-white house, don't get a Bouvier des Flandres. Between those fuzzy paws and his dirty beard, your walls and floors will never be the same. If you find the occasional dog hair in your casserole disgusting, skip the Alaskan Malamute. If you can't stomach a dog on the bed, you can't have a Whippet; they are born wanting to

DIANE LARATTA

be under the covers. If your idea of an active day is a slow stroll in the park, then a gleeful German Shorthaired Pointer may not be your cup of tea. Know thyself!

The bottom line is, Don't fall in love with a picture in a book. That's about as sensible (and successful) as selecting a spouse from a mail-order catalog. Think about how you live, then make an intelligent choice based on what you need. The most beautiful dog in the world is the one that fits into your lifestyle.

SPACE

Certain breeds need more space than others, and the amount isn't always based on the dog's physical size. An active Weimaraner needs more room to stretch than a more massive but calmer Saint Bernard. Some breeds require a yard or, if in an urban environment, a safe, conveniently located fenced area. If a breeder or rescue worker tells you the breed requires space that you don't have, accept it and move on. There are over four hundred breeds of dogs in the world; try not to get too attached to one.

COMMON SENSE

Common sense is a matter of experience more than intelligence. It can be acquired through study. To experienced dog people, it is common sense not to stare directly into the eyes of a strange dog, but until you learn that, how are you supposed to know?

TONI KAY

The common sense we want you to have relates to responsibility. More than ever, we all need to watch our dogs, both for their safety and the safety of others.

Dogs with children should be vigilantly watched, even dogs who are "good" with kids. All animals—including people—have a breaking point. You will only be able to see it coming if you can see it happening. Children should never be allowed to do anything to a dog that you would not allow them to do to an infant. Riding, chasing, hitting, scaring, annoying them when they sleep or eat all fall under the heading of harassment.

Dogs cannot be let out the door to wander free. This is dangerous for the dog and for other people. You are responsible for the damage your dog does, whether on purpose or by accident. Although we grew up in a world where both kids and dogs could wander free, that world no longer exists in most of the United States.

It is also common sense not to allow an animal to breed just for puppies or because it is natural. In a world where literally millions of animals are killed a year because they do not have a home, creating life is a serious responsibility. Do not breed unless you have researched genetic disease, studied canine development, can drop everything for seven weeks to tend the litter, are willing to take any animal you produce back at any time for any reason, and have a list of people already interested in your pups. People who love animals make sure no more are produced to go unloved, frightened, and confused to an early death. People who love animals neuter and spay their pets. That's just common sense.

When Is the Best Time to Get a Dog?

This is an individual decision, but there are a few things you might consider.

SEASON

Up north where we live, we do not recommend getting a puppy in winter. Housebreaking a puppy is harsh going in a sleet storm. Carrying a squirming pup down icy steps at one in the morning is no fun. Trying to don your winter gear before the pup urinates is a race against the clock.

Even more pressing is socialization, another of the responsibilities of rearing a dog. Getting a pup out and about—after your vet's okay—is critical to your companion's mental and behavioral development. If you put it off till the warmer months, you may miss an irreplaceable window of opportunity. The nervous, fearful, or aggressive dog your pup may now grow into is all your doing, but it will be the animal who suffers most.

HOLIDAYS

The holidays are a bad time to get a pet. Why? Most households are in an uproar. People are visiting, parties abound, and dangerous things like tinsel, chocolate, toxic plants, and candles are everywhere. Spur-of-the-moment thinking rules. If you have carefully considered this addition to your household, if you are ready to cope with winter socialization and housebreaking challenges, then gift-wrap a bowl, a toy, and a snapshot of the pup. Save the actual homecoming for a few days later, when all is cleared away and calm.

Never buy a pet for someone else as a gift. An animal is too great and personal a decision for someone else. If you are sure the recipient is interested, give a snapshot of the pup—if the breeder will allow it: Many good breeders will not allow such shenanigans, knowing that it rarely works out best for the pup.

VACATION

If everyone is normally out of the house all day, vacations are a good time to bring your new family member home. This allows you all to get to know each other a bit before the inevitable separation of work or school. Do yourself a favor, though: Stick to a similar schedule as your nonvacation one. Giving the dog all your attention during vacation, then suddenly isolating him when you go back to work is confusing and stressful for him and may cause him to develop separation anxiety. Instead, plan most of your interaction times for morning and evenings, allowing the day hours to be calmer ones. If you are going to have someone come in midday to care for the animal, have her start when you are at home. Not only does this foster a smoother transition for the dog, it also allows you to supervise this new caretaker.

MARY ANN SVIZENY

JUST BEFORE BABY

This is a common wish. Families want to get a puppy around the same time a baby arrives so the two can grow up together. This sounds like a good idea when every parental hormone you have is firing off in unison, but take our unhormonally influenced advice and don't do it!

Why not wait until after the baby? If you still have energy, attention, and time to spare a few months later, feel free. We've never had parents take us up on that suggestion. The beset time to add a dog to a family with children is when the children reach the age of some reason and a bare minimum of motor control—say, five or six years old.

Which One for Me?

Now that we have the *why* and the *when* conquered, let's go on to the *who* (or the *which*, depending on how you feel about dogs). Breed selection is covered in the rest of this book, but let's explore some other issues here.

MALE/FEMALE

Males are more aggressive? Females more loving? Not always, and especially not after neutering. In many breeds, it is the exact opposite. Neutered male Bouviers des Flandres and Australian shepherds can both be calmer and less reactive than females.

JOEL HOLLENBERG

males. Talk to breeders, rescue workers, and your vet before you make the decision of which sex you want or even if it makes any difference at all.

The rumor persists that males are harder to housebreak than females. We have not found this to be true. Neutering prevents many of the more obnoxious male dog traits from blossoming, like leg lifting, shin riding, and dogfighting. Every pet should be neutered at or before six months of age.

YOUNG/OLD – What age is best? First, never bring home a pup less than six weeks of age. Other than that, it's your choice.

YOUNG – Pups are adorable, affectionate, fuzzy, time-sucking, energy-eating, sleep-depriving beasts. Sarah is raising a pup at this moment. So far today she has gotten up at 4:30 A.M. for a quick potty run, taken the pup for two long walks, scrubbed out her crate, trimmed her nails, attended to a minor infection, removed several objects from her mouth (dangerous), inserted several safe objects into her mouth, supervised some social time with two of the adult dogs, and done a bit of training. It is now 10:00 A.M.

Would she change it? No, but it is a lot of work. Work that cannot be put off until a more convenient time.

VICKI CROKE

OLDER DOGS – The myth surrounding older dogs is that they won't bond to their new family. False! We have a German Shepherd male whom we acquired fully grown. He is marvelous. Endlessly devoted, as are many adopted adult dogs, he never voluntarily lets us out of his sight. Adults are comparatively settled. The energy levels, house-breaking, and chewing are all reasonably stable. Most adults arrive with a few issues of one kind or another. Our Shep-herd male came unhousebroken and uneducated about stairs, vacuums, and chewing furniture. None of these is-sues posed a big problem. He had all the rules down in about a month, though we still crate him when he is left alone. Some dogs take longer to train. Some come with more problems, some with fewer, but most of these problems are workable.

In general, do not take dogs that have been raised strictly in a kennel; it is roughly equivalent to adopting a child who has never stepped out of the house. If a dog isn't socialized as a youngster, you cannot do it effectively later. It is heartbreak-ing, but there are plenty of sweet, reasonably socialized dogs waiting for your love right now. Do not take any dog that is shy, skittish, or aggressive. Whatever age, or background, you want a happy, people-loving dog.

SIZE?

As mentioned before, the size of a dog can be misleading. Unless you have specific size needs, you are better off assessing your dog by temperament than by bulk. Say-

DIANA GONZALEZ

ing "I want a calm, easygoing dog in the city" is more useful than saying "I need a small apartment dog." A Miniature Pinscher is small in stature only. He will take up a giant-sized portion of time and energy.

That said, both extremes, tiny and huge, have their own charm. The vision of a thirty-seven-inch Great Dane stand-ing nobly by your side brings with it a sense of control, power, and safety few experiences can replicate. Yet the thought of cuddling a tiny toy puppy in the palm of your hands gets the parental juices of the toughest soul going. Fantasy aside, the realities are not nearly so romantic.

HUGE – Giant breeds are short-lived. If they see ten years old, it is an accomplishment. Health problems abound, and

even a minor temperament flaw that could be forgivable and perhaps even endearing in a smaller dog is a hazard in a big one.

Then there are the facts of living with them. When they walk up to your dinner table, they simply stand and survey the food. No spot on the counter is safe. Coffee tables will be cleared with one sweep of their tails. A joyful greeting bounce can knock you over. A happy hop up to lick your face can break a tooth or crack a facial bone. (Sarah lost half of her front tooth to an overly enthusiastic dog. And we know one owner who was sued when her large-breed dog gave a too-forceful hello that broke the cheekbone of a neighbor.)

Their size is unwieldy. Stretched out in the living room, they take up the space of a couch. They simply do not fit in the average car, nor can you easily buy a crate for one. You need to special-order it, then find a place in your home for a nearly four-foot-square cage.

None of this seems overwhelming if you are smitten by one of these wonderful giants. We have fallen hard for Great Danes, been enthralled by more than one Newfoundland, and dreamed of acquiring a Great Pyrenees. Yes, there are some drawbacks to their size, but those can be more than made up for by the enchanting personalities and interesting minds possessed by some giant breeds.

TINY – Smaller sounds easier than huge, right? Not really. While they won't break your teeth, they may break their own legs hopping off the bed or getting caught in a door by mistake. Stepping on a toy breed can cause serious injury to the dog. Trying to avoid stepping on one can cause injury to you.

They are prone to hypoglycemia (low blood sugar) and dehydration because they are so small. A bout of diarrhea that would be inconsequential for a normal-sized pup can mean hospitalization for a "teacup" poodle puppy. Dental problems are also significant, with retained puppy teeth and rotting adult teeth needing surgical attention. Again, their charms more than outweigh their downfalls, but anyone contemplating an extreme size should be aware of what is involved.

Basically, the ancestors of the dog were 35-to-45-pound wolves with pointed noses, erect ears, short coats, and long tails. The farther you get from that general model either in size or in shape, the more problems you are likely to discover.

How to Find Your Friend

Where you get your dog can mean the difference between a delightful experience and a painful or expensive one. But how do you know where to go? This chapter gives you detailed instruction about handling this emotional process.

A word to the wise: Remember, once you decide to buy a certain dog, it is a financial transaction. Even when a dog makes your heart sing, put your heart on hold and get your head involved. Use logic. Being an informed consumer is the best way to make this important purchase.

CHRISTINE M. PELLICANO

Researching a Breed

You've seen a breed you like the looks of, but you haven't got the whole story. How do you go about getting information on that breed? Today there are many resources available to you. All have their advantages and disadvantages.

RESOURCES

BOOKS – Sounds like a good idea, doesn't it? Well, it is and it isn't. Books published by breed clubs are useful for learning histories and standards of the dogs, but don't expect them to step up to the line about problems unique to their breed. Does

SARAH WILSON

a car dealer honestly tell you every little thing about a certain make or model of car? If you don't know a car has a rotten repair record or a notorious set of brakes, is that their problem?

Every breed has strengths and weaknesses. These unique characteristics are no insult to the breed. The real insult is keeping that information from people and then seeing the dogs misplaced as a result.

So where do you look? In books like this one. Books written by people with no vested interest in any one breed, who have long years of experience, and who want every dog to have the benefit of an appropriate home where their unique qualities will be cherished.

MAGAZINES – Magazines have become a much more honest source of information in the last few years. Genetic diseases and temperament tendencies are almost always noted. If they aren't, be suspicious. The most popular dog magazines are listed in this book's "Resources" section. For a few dollars a year, magazines can give you up-to-date, monthly information. You can also contact the publications and ask about articles on your breed.

THE INTERNET – The Internet is a spectacular source of information. By running a search on a breed and the acronym FAQ, which stands for "frequently asked questions," you can find a wealth of information as well as more resources to review. This is a huge boon and one well worth searching out even if you don't have a computer. Many public libraries now have computers you can use.

Sort through the information intelligently. Remember, anyone can post anything on the Internet. Again, if a breed comes out sounding more perfect than Rin Tin Tin, keep looking. Someone isn't telling the whole truth. We have seen some damaging advice posted on the Internet; we have also made some great friends and met some true dog experts. So keep your wits about you when you surf the Net.

If this dog's owner had learned about proper grooming, she would not have had to shave her Samoyed
SUZANNAH VALENTINETTI

VIDEOS – Videos can present similar problems as the breed books. If put out by a club, they are likely to make their dog sound better than sliced bread. They are wonderful resources for seeing what the dogs actually look like, but bear in mind that the dogs featured will be well-groomed, excellent specimens of the breed. Your

Pet owner's fantasy . . . reality . . . and more reality

dog may not look exactly like them. Videos are also expensive and seldom returnable, so they aren't our first choice as a selection resource.

VETERINARIANS, TRAINERS, GROOMERS – These folks are in the trenches with the dogs. They not only can tell you the breeds they recommend and the ones they don't, but they may also be able to steer you to local breeders who are doing a good job.

Sarah's dentist was researching dogs. He has three small children and a busy lifestyle. A canine deterrent sounded good, so he asked her about a Bull Terrier, a Rottweiler, or a Cane Corso. She told him that those large, powerful, assertive, independent breeds would be way too much dog for his level of experience and his lifestyle. If he wanted a dog who would bark at the door but lick the kids, need a good run every day but not too much focus the rest of the time, the three he mentioned were not the right breeds. She recommended a Labrador Retriever, a good watchdog and generally child-loving. By simply asking someone in the field, he saved himself a lot of time and potential aggravation.

RESCUE GROUPS – These hardy souls warrant their own section. If anyone is going to give you the straight poop about a breed, it is the long-suffering, truth-facing, hardworking rescue people. Almost every breed has an internal rescue network just for that breed. They care for the results of bad breeding, bad training, bad management, or, simply, bad choices, and they will usually give you the truth with both barrels. Remember, every breed was created for a reason and every breed has thousands of people devoted to it. The question is, Is this a breed you will be devoted to, and vice versa?

Names of rescue groups are available through the American Kennel Club, national and local breed clubs, and the Internet.

The Finalists

After reading this book, interviewing experts, and considering the decision thoughtfully, you come up with a couple of potential winners. How do you proceed?

SPEND SOME TIME

Now that you have narrowed the field, try to find a way to spend some time with actual dogs. Find a local breeder who has some time for you, or watch the breed at a dog show, or help out a rescue group on a Saturday. At the very least, find an owner willing to let you visit her dog(s). A trainer, groomer, or veterinarian should be able to help you locate such people. Most breed aficionados want to help a "newbie" learn about their beloved breed.

How to Read a Pedigree

Understanding a pedigree can be confusing at first. Here are a few tricks to make it easier.

➤ Boys on top, girls on the bottom.

➤ Read from left to right.

➤ Behind each name, slightly above and below it, are two more names. These are the dog's parents.

Pedigree abbreviations include:

➤ CH. = AKC Champion

➤ CAN. CH. = Canadian Champion

➤ V or VA = Highly rated German Dogs

Obedience Titles:

➤ CD = Companion Dog

➤ CDX = Companion Dog Excellent

➤ UD = Utility Dog

➤ OTCH = Obedience Trial Champion

AKC Agility Titles:

➤ NA, OA, AX, MX

AKC Hunting Titles:

➤ JH, SH, MH

Tracking Titles:

➤ TD, TDX, VST, CT

Others:

➤ TDI = Therapy Dog

➤ CGC = Canine Good Citizen

➤ TT/TC = Temperament Tested/Temperament Certified

➤ SCH I, II, III = Schutzhund Titles

LEARN ABOUT THE COMMITMENT

Speak to at least five people about the breed(s) you are considering. Ideally, that group would include two experienced breeders, a rescue worker, your veterinarian, and a trainer. Take notes. Ask about daily exercise requirements, health issues, coat care, shedding, classic breed temperament. Find out what type of home is best for the breed, how they are with kids, would the person recommend a male or a female, how much and what kind of training is recommended, and anything else you can think of.

These interviews can be done over the phone and can take as little as ten minutes. It is time well spent. Call breeders midweek. These busy folks are usually juggling work, family, and their dogs. Visit at their convenience, not yours. Keep in mind that people who compete with their dogs are often busy on the weekends. Introduce yourself, tell them you are considering their breed and have a few questions. Ask if they mind speaking with you. Most will be delighted. Before you hang up, ask them if there is anyone else you should speak to and what books or other resources they recommend.

Most Goldens will steal food, and this one is no exception
SUSAN RICHMAN

UNDERSTAND GENETIC DISEASE

Every dog carries genes for genetic disease. Every single one. You do too, for that matter. That's the problem — normal individuals carry the gene but do not have the disease itself. In that case, there is no way to see from the outside whether the gene is present. Rarely is there a test to find out if the dog carries the gene for a given disease. The best breeders can do is test the parents and the pups of previous litters from those parents for the problem itself. You can use those results as a guideline for your puppy's future health.

If a breeder has three generations free of a certain problem, you can be pretty sure your pup won't have it—pretty sure, not 100 percent sure. But if those tests were not done, you have no way of knowing. Zero. Which would you rather bet on: pretty sure or totally unknown?

Some puppy producers (breeders do research, producers don't) may not know the problems in their dogs. A classic example came up when a client's adorable Yorkshire Terrier, Echo, began to "skip." This skipping action is indicative of subluxating patellas or, more simply put, kneecaps that slip in and out of position. The dog raises its leg, or skips, to pop the kneecap back in place.

Assuming that any good breeder wants to know about inherited unsoundness, we gave her a friendly ring.

The conversation went something like this:

CHRISTINE M. PELLICANO

"We noticed Echo skipping, so we took her to the vet. The vet confirmed subluxating patellas."

"Oh, don't be silly," responded this breeder, a past officer of one of the breed's largest clubs. "She's skipping because she's happy. All my dogs skip. They are very happy little dogs."

That is not the only such tale we have. It will be up to you to research the breed you are interested in. One excellent way to find out the current problems in your breed is to look in the classified ads of a magazine like *Dog World*. Look for ads stating things like "hips cleared," "cardiac tested," "thyroid normal," which all show breeder commitment to health and physical soundness. Regardless of where in the country those breeders are located, call or write to them. If you write, please include a self-addressed stamped envelope. Ask them about these problems. Most people who get clearances are more than happy to chat about why they are necessary.

Another good sign is a breeder who trains her dogs for competition. People who enjoy agility, obedience, tracking, or herding are likely to put a high premium on structural and mental soundness. They will probably have a more complete understanding of their dogs' temperament than will people who do not work their dogs.

People who work their dogs know their dogs better

SARAH WILSON

Once you know about necessary health tests, do not buy a dog from someone who doesn't get them. You will hear many excuses on your journey; here are the top four:

"THOSE TESTS DON'T PROVE ANYTHING!" – While partially true, many tests do not prove whether the dog carries the problem, they do, however, prove that the dog does not have the problem. If enough dogs in a bloodline test free of that problem, then you can begin to hope that the family is free of the genetics for the problem.

"THOSE TESTS ARE TOO EXPENSIVE." – Hogwash. If people are charging hundreds of dollars for a puppy, they can afford to test. Most tests only have to be done once in the dog's life. Even the more expensive ones, like X-rays, which can cost a couple hundred dollars, are still only a small amount of one pup's value.

"MY LINE DOESN'T HAVE THOSE PROBLEMS." – Well, that's marvelous news! But if it were true, surely this person would be testing, then bronzing the results. How

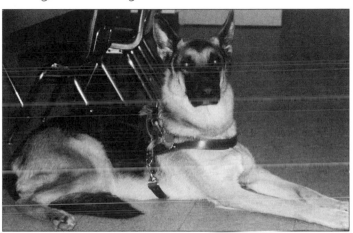

Good hips are important to all dogs, especially a working dog like Abner
RENEE EWING

does she know she doesn't have the problem if she doesn't test? Not every dog with hip dysplasia limps. If a breeder doesn't do the testing, she simply cannot make that statement. What you want to hear is, "I have tested for that problem for X generations and all my dogs have tested clear so far. Here are copies of the results."

"THAT PROBLEM IS IN THE BREED; THERE IS NO WAY TO AVOID IT." – Okay. Sometimes that is true, but whining about it won't help. Only through testing and selecting the best specimens, then breeding the healthiest dogs, will a breed fight its way clear of a problem.

How to Read an Ad

One recent ad for a popular breed read: "Pups . . . great coats, substantial bone, boxy heads, suitable for all your . . . needs." All my needs? How does that breeder know that? She spends lots of print telling me what her dogs look like but nothing about health or testing.

Compare that with this one: "Socialized puppies . . . to approved homes. . . . OFA, CERF, heart clearances. . . . Written guarantee!" This breeder cares about and knows the importance of socialization, is picky about where she places her dogs, gets health tests performed, and has a written contract. I think I'm in love.

Genetic problems are the breeder's nightmare. A breeder can do her best, spend hundreds of dollars, get all the clearances, and still come up with problems. That's the nature of the business.

Parental clearances on some diseases, like von Willebrand's disease, a bleeding disorder present in many breeds, do guarantee that your pup will be clear. In other cases, like hip dysplasia, they do not. But these clearances are an excellent indicator that a breeder is committed to attempting to avoid this and similar ills. That commitment is worth finding.

Crib Notes on Genetic Disease

Here are a few of the more common genetic problems. This listing is not close to being comprehensive because (a) we are not experts in this field; and (b) it's a really big field. If you want to learn more about genetic disease in general, or about one in particular, let us recommend the following:

- Ask your veterinarian.
- Contact the national breed club through the AKC (see "Resources"). Most will have educational material.
- Talk to a breeder who gets health clearances. She will probably be up on the breed's most common problems.
- Call any of the magazines listed and ask for past articles. They all have them.
- Get on the Web. A place like www.k9web.com has wonderful breed frequently asked questions (FAQ) that cover each breed's common genetic problems.

We thank Dr. Michael Moyer for assisting us with this section.

BLOAT

This condition is not yet well understood, but because some larger, deep-chested breeds and some lines within those breeds suffer more than others do, a genetic link is suspected. A few of the breeds that can be afflicted are Standard Poodle, German Shepherd Dog, Great Dane, Irish Wolfhound, Irish Setter, Golden Retriever, and Labrador Retriever.

Bloat is a life-threatening condition in which the stomach fills with gases and/or fluids that cannot be expelled. The stomach may also flip in place, damaging neighboring organs. Emergency surgery is needed, but it may not always save the dog's life.

Like so many large breeds, the Irish Setter is prone to bloat
BRIAN KILCOMMONS

CANCER

While not all cancers are inherited, some certainly are. Some breeds are prone to one type or another. Among the breeds prone to cancer are Boxer, Flat-Coated Retriever, Great Dane, Rottweiler, and, nowadays, Golden Retriever.

CARDIOMYOPATHY

This is an enlargement of the heart, which can lead to heart failure. Though this disease is progressive, medication can help in some breeds. Dogs of susceptible breeds, such as Doberman Pinscher, Great Dane, Irish Wolfhound, Cavalier King Charles Spaniel, German Shepherd Dog, and American Cocker Spaniel, should be tested clear for this problem before being bred. Testing should be repeated as the dog ages.

CATARACTS

There are several types of inherited cataracts, some of which form early in life and can lead to blindness. Breeding animals from breeds prone to this problem should be tested by the Canine Eye Registry Foundation (CERF) regularly. Some of the breeds affected are Australian Shepherd, Beagle, Bichon Frise, Chesapeake Bay Retriever, Golden Retriever, Labrador Retriever, Poodle (all sizes), Siberian Husky, and Staffordshire Bull Terrier.

It's hard to believe that dogs as active as Dobermans can have heart problems, but they can
SARAH WILSON

COLLIE EYE ANOMALY (CEA)

Common in Collies and present in some other herding breeds, CEA is discernible by a veterinary ophthalmologist at six to eight weeks of age. In one way or another, the back of the eye fails to develop normally. The effects range from none to blindness. Collie breeders have been working hard and more normal-eyed dogs are being produced every year. No Collie, Shetland Sheepdog, or Australian Shepherd should ever be bred before eye testing.

ELBOW DYSPLASIA (ED)

ROSEMARY GLADSTAR

More than one problem can cause elbow dysplasia but the result is the same, a malformed elbow. This can cause lameness, though some affected dogs do not limp. Dogs from susceptible breeds—such as Golden Retriever, German Shepherd Dog, Bouvier des Flandres, Bernese Mountain Dog, Bullmastiff, Newfoundland, to name a few—should have elbows certified with the OFA or GDC before breeding.

ENTROPION

A fairly common problem in some breeds, just a few of which are the American Cocker Spaniel, Shih Tzu, Pug, Poodle (all sizes), Papillon, Labrador Retriever, English Springer Spaniel, Golden Retriever, and Bulldog. Entropion is when the edges of the eyelid (and thus the eyelashes) roll inward, irritating the eyeball. Affected pups either grow out of it or can be surgically corrected.

EPILEPSY

Causing seizures, epilepsy is not well understood. The seizures are sometimes random and mild, sometimes frequent and hard to control. Drugs that control epilepsy are available, but they do not work on all dogs. Treatment can be frustrating. Some of the breeds wrestling with the problem are Welsh Springer Spaniel, Poodle (all sizes), Australian Shepherd, German Shepherd Dog, Belgian Sheepdog, Belgian Tervuren, American Cocker Spaniel, Beagle, and Shetland Sheepdog.

HIP DYSPLASIA (HD)

The bane of many a breeder's existence, this is a problem in the hip joint. The joint is not well formed or it could be loose; either way it leads to problems. Pain tolerance differs dog to dog; some dogs handle horrible hips with ease, while others limp with even a mild case. Although not normally tested, some small dogs are proving to be dysplastic when X-rayed. Various treatments exist. In most, but not all, cases, the dog can be made reasonably comfortable. With the exception of a few sighthounds, almost every large breed struggles with HD. Some of the worst hit are Old English

Sheepdog, Saint Bernard, German Shepherd Dog, Akita, Golden Retriever, Labrador Retriever, and Bulldog.

LEGG-CALVES PERTHES DISEASE

Another problem that causes rear-end lameness, LCPD hounds many of the small breeds, including American Cocker Spaniel, Australian Terrier, Chinese Crested, Cairn Terrier, Miniature Pinscher, and West Highland White Terrier.

PROGRESSIVE RETINAL ATROPHY (PRA)

As the name implies, in this disorder the retina of the eye degenerates, which leads to compromised vision, then blindness. Dogs used for breeding should be CERF (Canine Eye Registry Foundation) approved. As PRA can develop late in life, breeding stock should be rechecked at least every two years throughout their lives. PRA is present in many breeds. Here are a few: all the retrievers, Irish Setter, both Cocker and Springer Spaniels, Portuguese Water Dog, Samoyed, Siberian Husky, Soft-Coated Wheaten Terrier, Poodle (all sizes), Tibetan Terrier, Shetland Sheepdog, Collie, Shiba Inu.

JOAN TORTORELLO

SEBACEOUS ANDENITIS (SA)

A skin disease that can lead to baldness. This mysterious problem is turning up in more breeds seemingly yearly. It's been proven to have a genetic basis, but why it happens and how to control it are still unknown. As the problem is not always visible to the naked eye, a skin-punch biopsy is necessary. SA can develop later in life, so skin-punch biopsies need to be repeated. More breeds seem to be developing this problem, but it is most prevalent in Poodle (all sizes), Vizsla, Samoyed, Lhasa Apso, Old English Sheepdog, Akita, German Shepherd Dog, and Golden Retriever.

Giving Back

You wanted a healthy dog. You searched high and low to find one. Congratulations!

Now you have an obligation to the breeder. Keep her informed of any and all health issues that arise. Not in an angry way but in an "I thought you'd like to know . . ." manner.

If she sends out a questionnaire, fill it out. If she calls you, answer truthfully. If you promised to get a health test done, do it. It is your way of helping her continue to improve her breeding program. It is your way of supporting the breed you have now come to love.

SUBLUXATING PATELLAS (SLIPPING PATELLAS, SLIPPING KNEECAPS, LUXATED PATELLA, PATELLAR LUXATION)

There are a lot of names for a trick knee. The kneecap, or patella, lies in grooves in the leg bones. If those grooves are shallow, the kneecap can slide out of position. If it does, that is called subluxation. Usually not painful, many dogs can live comfortably without intervention. Surgery, which deepens those grooves thereby eliminating the problem, is often successful. OFA now evaluates knees, so look for OFA clearances on this problem. Many breeds can have this problem; a few of those breeds are Jack Russell Terrier, Yorkshire Terrier, Maltese, Chihuahua, Italian Greyhound, Papillon, Pomeranian, Shih Tzu.

GWENN BARBA

VON WILLEBRAND'S DISEASE (VWD)

A single blood test will show how well a dog's blood clots. The test can be done at any age. With this problem, a dog's blood does not clot well, or may not clot at all. Depending on the severity of the problem, the dog may live a long life or an unnaturally short one. Some of the breeds affected are Doberman Pinscher, Great Dane, French Bulldog, Shih Tzu, Poodle (all sizes), and Shetland Sheepdog.

Finding a Breeder

Now that you know which breed(s) you're interested in and what problems exist, how do you find a good breeder? That's a fine question. As far as we can tell, your best approach is a combination of research and prayer.

Word of mouth is excellent. Go to local shows and training clubs. If you find dogs you like, ask where they came from. (Also, if you find dogs you don't like, find out where they came from.) Call veterinarians and trainers for referrals.

For many breeds, you may not find a local breeder. Then what do you do? Write to the national club and ask for a breeder list. Or call advertisers in large dog magazines. We've found lovely dogs that way, but keep in mind that anyone can advertise in these publications. We've also come across some truly unethical people.

What you are looking for is a committed hobby breeder. Steer clear of people who make their entire living off their dogs. We've never met one who had the consumer's best interest in mind; many did not even appear to have the dog's best interests in mind. Also beware of people who breed more than one breed.

Ask how many litters a breeder has a year. Anyone with more than two or three

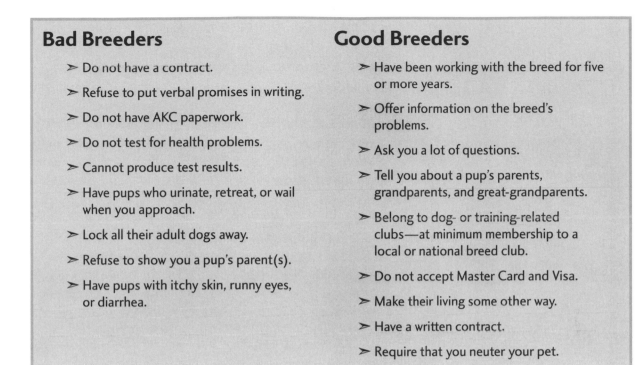

Bad Breeders

➤ Do not have a contract.

➤ Refuse to put verbal promises in writing.

➤ Do not have AKC paperwork.

➤ Do not test for health problems.

➤ Cannot produce test results.

➤ Have pups who urinate, retreat, or wail when you approach.

➤ Lock all their adult dogs away.

➤ Refuse to show you a pup's parent(s).

➤ Have pups with itchy skin, runny eyes, or diarrhea.

Good Breeders

➤ Have been working with the breed for five or more years.

➤ Offer information on the breed's problems.

➤ Ask you a lot of questions.

➤ Tell you about a pup's parents, grandparents, and great-grandparents.

➤ Belong to dog- or training-related clubs—at minimum membership to a local or national breed club.

➤ Do not accept Master Card and Visa.

➤ Make their living some other way.

➤ Have a written contract.

➤ Require that you neuter your pet.

litters a year is suspect. (The exception to this is toy breeders. Because the litters are routinely tiny, they tend to breed a bit more frequently.) Raising pups is time-consuming, and doing it right is exhausting. You want your pup to have gotten plenty of love and personalized attention.

One would hope that someone producing pups would know about their breed. Sadly, this is not always so. We still see ads for Brittany Spaniels, even though the name officially became simply Brittany in 1982.

Beware of people who sell undesirable traits as "rare" and therefore expensive. Such "treasures" include long-haired Akitas, particolored Poodles, oversized Dobermans, and mismarked Great Danes. There is nothing wrong with these individuals as companions, but they deviate from AKC standard and should not cost more than a correct specimen.

Beware the backyard breeder as well. These people own one maybe two dogs that they love. They do little or no showing, training, or other canine activities. They do not belong to any breed or training clubs. They do not know about or get genetic clearances. Few are familiar with the breed standard or the pedigree of their dogs. Their reason for breed-

If you can find someone as ethical and careful as Mary you'll be lucky indeed
MIKE STEIGERWALD

ing: "My Spot is such a nice dog." Spot may be sweet as pie, but if breeding were simply a matter of nice dogs producing nice dogs, the world would be full of only nice dogs.

When Brian purchased his Rottweiler, Beau, from Mrs. Muriel Freeman, the grand dame of Rottweilers, he got written evaluations and pictures of three generations of ancestors. Mrs. Freeman wrote up a list of traits that his puppy was likely to have given his ancestry: an impressive package.

A conscientious breeder does not actively breed a double-digit number of bitches. Do not count retired matrons or up-and-coming stars in this group, please. A good breeder wants you to come and see her stock at a mutually convenient time. One Great Dane breeder replied to Sarah's request to visit with "Come and see my dogs? That's a huge inconvenience! This is not a petting zoo!" Sarah thanked her as she hung up. Anyone who is hesitant about allowing you to see her dogs is not someone you want to deal with.

Rescue Groups

Most rescue groups are inundated with dogs that need homes. Often, dog/owner mismatch is the primary reason.

"I didn't know a Great Pyrenees would get so big!"

"Do all Springers need so much exercise?"

"He barks and barks: Is that normal for an Elkhound?"

"There's hair everywhere! You have to take this Shepherd."

Many of these dogs will make terrific companions in a home that appreciates them. Rescue groups are normally quite tough on temperament issues. After all, they do their breed no favors by placing aggressive animals. In most cases, the available dogs are either held by the owner for placement or fostered out in homes. This is a resource to consider if you want a slightly older puppy or dog.

Shelters

SARAH WILSON

These are similar to rescue groups, only all the dogs are kenneled. Putting a house pet in such a situation is both stressful and disorienting. You will not always see the dog's real personality—the good and the not so good—until he has been home for a week or longer.

There is no such thing as a no-kill shelter. There are only "We kill very few and make others kill the rest" shelters. While some do an excellent job caring for the dogs, others house too many animals for too long, leading to high levels of stress, disease, and aberrant behavior.

Sadly, in this country millions of excess animals are killed every year. Do not blame the shelter for this. It isn't their fault. They are only doing what has to be done. Being angry with them for killing the dogs is like being angry with a mortician during a plague. "How could he be burying so many people? That is disgusting!" He didn't create the problem. He's just sweeping up the mess.

Most shelters go out of their way to keep sweet, adoptable dogs alive for as long as possible. Go to those places. Those dogs need your help the most.

Pet Stores

Don't. Yes, we know the puppies are cute. True, it isn't their fault they are stuck in cages. But when you buy from pet stores, you support an industry that does not support the dogs. Pet-store dogs rarely come from health-tested stock. You have no clue as to the parents' temperaments or how the puppy was raised.

Many times you'll pay more for a puppy-mill pup than for a top-quality pup from the nation's top breeders. In addition, the pups are stressed, all too often sick, and in some cases extremely hard to housebreak. Some pups are removed from their mothers much too young, leading to unavoidable serious temperament problems later.

Perfect Puppy Parents

Mother is calm and friendly. Some breeds are more protective than others, but by the time the pups are six weeks old all females should be able to greet strangers politely somewhere in her home.

Mother looks healthy. Unless she is a sighthound, she should not be bony. She should be shiny, clean, and well groomed, with toenails clipped and ears spotless. Her coat should be shiny.

Parents are health-tested—and copies of health-test results are readily available for you to review.

Parents have a title or two; the easiest are the CGC (Canine Good Citizen) and the TT (Temperament Test). Although not a guarantee that the dog is stable, these are good signs. Others might be a CD (Companion Dog) or TDI (Therapy Dog). They may or may not be a champion. A championship shows beauty and breeder commitment, but it does not reflect a breeder's health or temperament goals.

Of course pet stores are not stupid. They know the public is onto the puppy-mills horror. Now they claim their puppies "come from breeders." Oh? No ethical breeder would ever hand over a precious puppy to a stranger to sell to another stranger who only needs a credit card that clears to purchase it. Never. People who allow their pups to be sold in a pet store may well produce puppies, but they are not reputable breeders.

If you fall in love with a puppy in the window, find out its breed then go call a breeder or rescue group. Do not give your money to the puppy-mill industry and underwrite more sloppy breeding, inhumane rearing conditions, and puppy deaths due to stress and disease, not to mention keeping the animals in tiny, toyless cages that are the canine equivalent of solitary confinement.

Making Your Choice

You have done your homework and found a breeder you like, who tests her dogs, who thinks you can provide a great home, has a litter and actually has one or two pups still available. Good work. Now what?

VISITING

If possible, visit the breeder. Bring a present and your wits. Look around. Does she have clean, friendly dogs in the house with her? If she has dogs in kennels—and she may well—is the fencing in good shape? Are the runs clean? Are the dogs clean and healthy looking? Are they friendly? A trophy case packed with ribbons is impressive, but not if it isn't backed up by healthy, friendly, well-cared-for dogs.

MEET THE MOTHER

Both parents gave their genes to your pup, but mom has the biggest influence on temperament because she raises them. A nice, relaxed, people-friendly mother is more likely to have the same kind of puppy.

If you see anything less than this, say thanks and leave. Do not accept excuses like "I didn't get a chance to run her today" or "I never got her out much as a puppy." Maybe that's true, maybe it isn't, but don't bet the next ten years of your life on someone else's say-so, especially when that person is trying to sell you something.

The mother has a profound effect on a pup's future temperament

SARAH WILSON

PUPPY SELECTION BASICS

In many cases, the breeder will pick a puppy for you. This is usually fine. After all, she knows them best. Occasionally, though, the breeder may be making her choice according to which puppy is not a good show prospect rather than which one is a good companion prospect. How can you tell? First off, ask her why she picked this pup for you. If she talks about the temperament being perfect for your needs, that is good. If she talks about his tail set being a little low and his front being a bit east-west (don't worry what that means; for your purposes it means she isn't thinking about his temperament first), that is not a good sign. He may still be a terrific pup for you, but you'll need to do a little testing first.

Before we discuss resources for puppy testing, let's talk about the common ways people pick pups. Here are the top three pups people select. First: the adorable one with the cute face, markings, ears, etc. Second: that quiet one looking so sad in the corner. Third: the bold one who is growling while he is tugging on my shoelaces—he seems to have picked me!

All those puppies are appealing, but each is the wrong choice. Do not select by color or markings. Sure, those are easy to get attached to, but they aren't the least bit relevant in your day-to-day life with your dog. If it comes down to two equally good pups, then by all means indulge your whimsy. But whimsy is the last thing—not the first thing—you indulge.

How about that "sad" one in the corner? Another poor choice. A companion puppy destined for your home should be happy, relaxed, and confident. Withdrawn pups may have a hard time handling stress, be genetically suspicious of people, or not be feeling well. Any one of those things is a bad sign. Skip that pup.

The bold one gnawing on your arm—isn't he perfect? Yes, for a competition

How to Interview a Breeder

If you begin the conversation with "I'm looking for a happy, healthy family pet," you'll find most people have just what you are looking for! If you want to know the real deal, ask the breeder questions, then listen. We like to ask open-ended questions, like: "What are your top three breeding priorities?" "What type of temperament are you breeding for?" "Good" is not an answer. A "good" temperament for a police K9 is not a "good" temperament for a family dog. "What are your dogs' strengths?" Also, get references—at least a couple of professionals (veterinarians or trainers are good) and a few previous pet buyers.

home that wants an energetic and assertive dog. Raised improperly, this pup may mature into aggression. Leave him to the people who have the experience, time, energy, and training skills to direct this puppy toward acceptable behavior.

Where is your pup? He may not stick out because he is a middle-of-the-road kind of guy. He isn't climbing up your chest or hiding under the chair. He comes over happily when you clap your hands and praise him, waiting (reasonably) patiently or wandering off when you ignore him.

Which one do you pick?

CHRISTINE M. PELLICANO

He is calm and relaxed. He is friendly but not cloying; playful but not wild. He may not win your heart the way his more demanding or neurotic siblings do, but he is easier to love in your home. We promise. You'll never be sorry you chose him.

Even if you think you want an active dog, choose a calm puppy. Even the calmest pup is active enough for 95 percent of American families.

The best way to discover which puppy would work best for you is to do a few puppy tests. There are many different ways to test a pup or a litter of pups. The process is a bit more than we can discuss in this book. If you would like to learn more, here are a few excellent resources:

Good Owners, Great Dogs
by Brian Kilcommons and Sarah Wilson

Puppy Personality Profile
by Jack Volhard and Wendy Volhard

Understanding Puppy Testing
by Suzanne Clothier

Choosing an Adult Dog

When you are considering an adult dog, get as much information on the dog's background as you can. People giving up their dog for adoption are notoriously dishonest about their reasons. They hope their dog won't be killed, so they say things like "We're moving," or "Our child has allergies," when what they mean is that the dog is out of control, not housebroken, etc. In short, shelters may not have the whole story. Rescue groups usually take extensive histories, but if they have rescued a dog from a shelter, they may be in the dark as well.

The best people to talk to in a shelter are the people who tend the dogs. The kennel workers know these dogs and can point you in the right direction. Many shelters are now temperament-testing animals right in the shelter, which makes appropriate selection easier. There are wonderful dogs available at almost every shelter that will blend in with your family with little effort.

BOB & KAREN ARENDS

If you want a certain breed, let the local shelter know. Stop by once a week to show them you are serious. They are usually eager to help.

Seeing a stressed dog's real temperament when confined at a shelter can be tricky. Consider hiring a local trainer to help you. They should be able to assess temperament and are usually thrilled when someone calls before they get a dog.

What Is Temperament Testing?

Temperament testing is a series of exercises that give insight into a dog's or puppy's personality. Most of these "tests" focus on two general areas: a dog's relationship to people and his reaction to various stressors. By assessing an animal's relationship with people it is possible to predict whether he has dominant or submissive tendencies, is drawn to people or is independent, likes children or is unsure. By subjecting him to stress, future strengths and weaknesses can be anticipated. A dog frightened by a set of keys dropping on the floor may well find a household of noisy toddlers overwhelming. A dog who relaxes when held on his side may well be easier to groom and handle. The books we list in this chapter have excellent testing information in them but the best idea of all is to enlist the help of an experienced person.

Selecting an adult dog is an art in itself. To learn more, read these fine books:

Adoption Option, Rubenstein and Kalina, 1996

Mutts: America's Dogs, Kilcommons and Capuzzo (Though the book addresses mixed breeds, the testing of adult dogs in the same, regardless of ancestry.)

Save That Dog!, Palika, 1997, Howell Books

Good Luck

Armed with all this knowledge, you are now ready for the happiest of hunts. Your companion is out there waiting for you with a wagging tail and a happy grin. Go find him—or her!

Your Dog –
Then and Now

Humans created breeds for a specific purpose. That purpose, no matter how long ago it originated, still influences the dogs today. Through the years, we have found people both fascinated and surprised by the clear connections between past purpose and present-day behavior.

This next chapter is an overview of different function-based groups of dogs, the tasks they were bred for, and how their history affects them today.

A disclaimer: These are generalizations based on our forty-five combined years of experience. For every few dogs that fit the description, there may be an exception. Each dog is an individual. Nonetheless, we bet you'll recognize dogs you know in these descriptions. Remember, there are no perfect breeds, but there are probably some breeds that are perfect for you.

It's not hard to see that this little guy is into everything
DIANE HACKE

Terriers:
Cairn Terrier, West Highland White Terrier, Norwich and Norfolk Terriers

When people learned to farm they needed, for the first time, to house large stores of grain. With such an abundant food source, the rodent population multiplied. Cats were good, but when rats raided the rations, weasels were in the henhouse, and gophers were ruining our fields, we needed reinforcements. We needed terriers.

Hard-nosed, hard-fighting, hard-living dogs, most terriers would be beer-guzzling, bar-fighting, football-playing, barbell-lifting guys if they were human.

CHRISTINE SWINGLE

Imagine a small dog going down a hole in pursuit of some panicked animal. Many feet below the surface, the animal and the dog have it out. The animal is fighting for its life—biting and scratching for all he is worth. The terrier takes the pain and keeps on going. In fact, the pain spurs him on. Humans call that a "game attitude"; terriers call it just plain fun.

Once terriers went into burrows, they often found it impossible to get back out. That's why they bark. The owners located their terriers by the yapping, then dug them free. All the silent terriers perished long ago down various beasties' holes. What kind of dog does this work create?

FEARLESS

Here's a dog that is not intimidated by much. A larger dog? Ha! The bigger they come, the better. A truck? He'll try to stop it. They are courageous to the point of brashness. As a terrier owner, it is your job to protect them from themselves by keeping them safely contained in a secure fence or on-lead. Not every terrier will start a fight, but few will walk away from one.

PREDATORY

Terriers chase. If not trained otherwise, squirrels, mice, even cats are fair game. Once they are launched, they will often fail to respond to a command until the chase is completed; that might be across a four-lane highway. They are not to be trusted off-lead.

EXCAVATOR

If you don't mind craters, this is not a problem. Some people give their diggers a designated digging zone, others resign themselves to potholes, others confine the dog in a dig-proof kennel, and more do not leave their dogs outside unattended. One thing is for sure: Punishing a terrier for digging is about as effective as punishing him for breathing.

LOUD

"Barkiness" ranges in all breeds, but for more than a few terrier breeds, barking is simply what they do. They bark when they are excited, frustrated, annoyed, anticipatory, bored, or happy. Redirecting barking by telling the dog to lie down or to go get a toy can help, but don't expect to get silence. If you want a nonvocal dog, don't get a terrier.

TOUGH WHEN EXCITED

This is a tricky one. It isn't that they like pain, it's just that once they are stimulated, they don't react to it in a "normal" way. A terrier can be quite sensitive when calm. At those times a firm tone of voice is effective. But once your dog is spitting canine cuss words at the neighbor's dog, even strong corrections may fail to interrupt the behavior. In fact, they are likely to spur the dog into a greater frenzy.

COMMON PROBLEMS – Barking, jumping, aggression (all types), leg lifting, digging, fighting, chasing other animals, hyperactivity, running off.

GOOD HOMES – Households with older children and adults with time for daily romping. Training should be viewed as a spiritual experience where the process is as important as the goal. A sense of humor combined with a will of steel is mandatory for a terrier owner. If you're impatient, controlling, or self-serious, get another type of dog. Stay calm, be persistent, and it will all work out . . . eventually. Never give up; your terrier won't!

Retrievers:
Labrador Retriever, Golden Retriever, Chesapeake Bay Retriever

Retrievers, not surprisingly, were created to retrieve. Their job is to sit by a hunter all day, wait for game to fly by, wait till the gun is fired, wait till the game is downed, then, on command, retrieve that game. When they bring the bird back, they should not make a mark on it. At times, a retriever cannot even see where the bird fell. In these instances, they follow their owner's commands, often at a great distance. Classically, retrievers work in cold, sometimes icy, water but they can also work in heavy brush. What sort of dog does this job produce?

DOUG ANTUNA

TOUCH INSENSITIVE

If a retriever were a "sensitive" dog, she would never leap into cold waters or break through heavy brush to retrieve, nor would she sit contentedly waiting for another chance to work as icicles formed on her coat. These physically tough dogs are normally tolerant of children's behavior, though that is not license to allow harassment. They can be stoic, not showing signs of an injury. Physically forceful training methods are not as effective as techniques that engage their excellent minds and strong desire to please.

SOUND INSENSITIVE

Sitting close to a hunter when guns go off requires a dog who thinks nothing of loud noise. Sound-insensitive dogs do not respond to yelling and are usually calm around noisy children. Fireworks or thunderstorms do not bother them. Nowadays, with the increased popularity of retrievers, overbreeding has produced all kinds of deviations from the norm, including dogs that are frightened by loud sounds.

FRIENDLY

A good retriever will hunt for most anyone. Aggression was of no use in these dogs. Growling at a hunting buddy or mauling the ducks were not useful qualities in a working retriever. Just about all Goldens and most Labs will follow anyone with a tennis ball. These dogs are usually safe with children's friends and guests. You can send a friend safely into your home by himself. This does not apply to the Chesapeake, who can be, and often is, a one-person protective dog.

ORAL

For a retriever, nirvana is just a stick, or a sock, or a ball away. Every event is more meaningful, every encounter more pleasant, if they have something in their mouths. If nothing is at hand, then your hand will do. This is not aggression but a retriever's instinctual, genetic oral need. Early training can easily direct this need to more acceptable objects.

COMMON PROBLEMS – Sins of enthusiasm: mouthing, jumping, pulling on lead, and chewing. Chesapeakes can be territorial, possessive, and aggressive toward other dogs.

Field Bred or Show Bred?

In general, dogs bred for top competition in any field can be too intense, assertive, and high energy to make easygoing companions. In sporting breeds, watch out for field trial champions. As one breeder proudly told a friend, "My dogs are so calm you can even let them in the house."

Other activities that can create high-demand and high-energy dogs are competition obedience, Schutzhund, and Ring Sport. If you can find lines that do these things AND other things—fine. But breeding solely for these competitions will not usually create good pets.

GOOD HOMES – People who have time for several exercise periods a day. Time must be available for regular training sessions, as these guys can be quite physical until taught to control themselves. Don't expect them to handle unsupervised freedom in the house until after two years of age.

Spaniels:
American Cocker Spaniel, English Cocker Spaniel, English Springer Spaniel, Welsh Springer Spaniel

Spaniels were bred to run in front of hunters and flush (scare) the birds into flight. Unlike pointers, who staunchly hold still until the hunter catches up, the spaniel bounces gleefully about, looking for quarry. It does the hunter no good to have the birds take flight out of range of his gun, so spaniels are supposed to stay close by at all times. Ideally, once the bird takes flight, the spaniel will sit while the shot is fired. When the bird falls, a command from his owner sends the spaniel to retrieve the bird. At least that's how it is supposed to work. And what kind of a dog does this work produce?

KATHLEEN WELLS

COMPLIANT
Staying close to the hunter takes some self control and willingness to please on the dog's part. Correct spaniels are generally eager to make you happy. They joyfully obey with no concerns about who is or isn't in charge; they just know they aren't. Good spaniels are rarely aloof or difficult. Most take well to training.

FRIENDLY
Not selected for any form of aggression, a correct spaniel is a happy dog who loves everyone equally. Though popularity has ravaged both the American Cocker and the English Springer, creating animals with horrible aggression problems, good specimens of both breeds are still some of the nicest dogs around. A good spaniel is well worth the trouble to locate.

GREGARIOUS
These are not one-man dogs. Have cookie, will follow. If you want a dog who will love your kids and the neighbor's kids and that strange kid he just met, find a nice spaniel. If you want a dog to love you and ignore all others, look elsewhere.

COMMON PROBLEMS – Hyperactivity, shyness, submissive wetting (American Cockers), dominance aggression and possessiveness (American Cockers and English Springers).

GOOD HOMES – Owners who have time for a good romp or a couple of long walks a day. Time and inclination for daily grooming. Training and socialization necessary, but these are rarely problems in a nice spaniel. A carefully bred specimen is wonderful for all ages.

Pointers:
Vizsla, Weimaraner, German Shorthaired Pointer, Brittany

Created to run, often covering more than ten miles over rugged terrain in a few hours, Pointers worked independently and at a distance from the hunter. To do their job well, they had to be single-minded, and remain undistracted by other sights and smells. Several of the pointing breeds were also expected to protect the hunter's possessions and family. This being the case, what can we expect from a pointer as a pet?

MASON ROSE

GREAT ENDURANCE
First, because they were bred to run long distances, pointers have wonderful endurance. If you jog a few miles a day, or think that throwing a ball for forty-five minutes twice a day is fun, consider these breeds. Otherwise, look elsewhere.

PHYSICALLY TOUGH
Because they had to run through brush and briar, they are physically tough. They think nothing of pinning you against a wall when saying hello or shoving you out of the way as they leap out the door. This translates into training time for you.

SINGLE-MINDED
Remember that single-mindedness? When training a pointer, you have to be more determined than they. You also have to be a step ahead of them mentally, and that's not always as easy as it sounds.

COMMON PROBLEMS – Hyperactivity, jumping, pulling on lead, overprotectiveness, chasing other animals, running off, destructive chewing, aggression.

GOOD HOMES – Experienced dog owners with the time, interest, and energy for all the exercise and training these breeds require. Generally good for children, though may knock over smaller kids in their exuberance. Too much for people who don't like a strong, active, physical, directed dog. Patience, firmness, and absolute consistency are mandatory. Early training is a must!

Setters:
Irish Setter, English Setter, Gordon Setter

Another athletic gun-dog group, setters share a similar history with pointers but tend to be a bit more pliable and a lot more clownish. They were not expected to be guards. All these breeds require grooming time.

ACTIVE
The English and the Gordon need daily runs, particularly when young. But neither is especially prone to hyperactivity unless they come from field lines. If they do, expect them to be kinetic, hard-muscled running machines. The Irish Setter is another matter, needing several long runs daily, and even then, do not expect long periods of calm behavior.

SOFTER THAN A POINTER
Most setters are owner-sensitive; they desperately want to please you. Gordons can be determined and strong-willed, but most come around with training.

COMMON PROBLEMS – Same as the pointing breeds, but fewer aggression problems.

GOOD HOMES – People of all ages who have the time for the grooming, training, and exercise that is critical for these dogs. People aggravated by constant activity in the house may find the Irish or some field-bred setters annoying. On the whole, though, we don't see many setters in for training, which usually means they are relatively problem-free.

CHRISTINE M. PELLICANO

Flock Guards:
Great Pyrenees, Kuvas,
Komondor, Akbash

When we humans started amassing large numbers of animals, such as flocks of sheep, we issued an open invitation to local predators to come get the goods. Sheep—slow, easy to find, abundant—were a predator's dream come true.

With our flocks threatened, we decided to fight fire with fire. We created a large predator of our own to help out. To protect our flocks further, we bred these guardians to look as much like sheep as a dog can. Large, white, and shaggy, our canine stealth weapons blended into the flock seamlessly until a threat arose. Then out they came, barking furiously, defending against—but not pursuing—the threat. It is no help to the shepherd if the dog chases an individual wolf all over creation while the rest of the wolf pack attacks the flock. What kind of dog does this history create?

CHRISTINE M. PELLICANO

INDEPENDENT

These dogs act on their own. When your friend Bob jumps out from behind a door to "surprise" you, do not expect your dog to wait for your command to act, nor will he stop in midair on command. These dogs are serious; they need extraordinary amounts of training to be responsive in a moment of perceived crisis. Of this group, the Great Pyrenees is the softer and easier-to-control breed.

LOUD

Many of these dogs bark, especially at night and not always at anything you can put your finger on. Some people suspect the dog is posting an auditory Beware: Guard Dog on Duty! sign.

DO NOT WANDER OFF TERRITORY

Normally not wanderers, these dogs want to patrol their territory daily. If your boundaries are made clear early in his life, your dog will respect them. If you allow him to form his own, he may include parts of neighboring properties. A secure fence is your best ally.

POWERFUL

These are huge dogs with little sense of humor about their work. Amazingly intelligent animals, if they are not socialized extensively, trained persistently, and managed responsibly, they can be a hazard.

SINGLE-FAMILY DOGS

Once these dogs have bonded to you, they have little use for anyone else. Again, Pyrs are the most social of this group, but in general they will have eyes only for you. This may sound flattering, but it is a great deal of responsibility.

AGGRESSIVE

Built to protect, these dogs will warn with a bark if given a chance. But if a threat appears in their home, they will act. Don't send your neighbor into the house for a beer—not, at least, if you like him. These dogs can also be fierce if any strange dog enters their territory.

COMMON PROBLEMS – Aggression of all types, difficult to control, barking, digging.

GOOD HOMES – Experienced dog people who want a canine project. Flock guardians are not casual dogs but high-maintenance animals that need an endless amount of socialization and training to be their best.

The exception to this is the Great Pyrenees, who, after years of breeding for show, is generally a kinder, gentler dog than his more primitive counterparts. If you want a white mountain of fur and are ready for a serious commitment, the Pyrenees is your best choice.

Kuvasok and Komondorok are amazing dogs—loyal, intelligent, and focused—but they are not appropriate for a casual home looking for an easy companion dog.

Scent Hounds:
Beagle, Basset Hound, Bloodhound

Scent hounds normally hunt in groups and are housed together outside. These animals are chosen for their single-minded ability to trail game, their melodious voices by which the hunters follow their progress, and their ability to live in close quarters. How does this history translate into present-day behavior?

SUPERB SCENTING ABILITY

Greetings from this group usually entail the sniffing of every available inch of your body. Bred for their scenting skills, these dogs live in a world we can never fully un-

DIANE LARATTA

derstand. With a nasal ability many thousands of times, possibly a million times, better than ours, they live amidst rich, apparently fascinating smells. Expect their noses to be on the ground most of the time.

NASAL-RELATED DEAFNESS

When the nose is working, the hearing usually isn't. This kind of single-mindedness was perfect for the hunt, but it can be frustrating in the home. A good fence and a strong leash are your main methods of controlling this trait. Sure, you can train them and you might even get some control when the dog is close at hand. But if your Beagle stumbles across a fresh rabbit trail fifty feet away from you, don't expect him to come when called.

GARBAGE EATING

That fine nose must give them a fine palate, because scent hounds have a profound joy of eating. Dining options may include tidbits from your dinner plate, garbage can, or the sidewalk. Some of these breeds can be possessive of their food; teaching food-bowl etiquette early, as well as the commands "Out" and "Leave it," can prevent problems from developing. Positive, food-based training methods work well for these dogs. Getting "tough" with them can put you into a battle royal.

HOUSEBREAKING CHALLENGES

For whatever reason, many individuals in this group can be a challenge to housebreak. The best approach is to stick to a feeding and walking schedule, supervise carefully, and do not allow a pup freedom in the house when you are gone. Punishing mistakes tends to make matters worse. Instead, use food to reward going in the right place at the right time; treats and kindness will help build good habits quickly.

LOW DOG-TO-DOG AGGRESSION

Normally, these breeds can be labeled "Plays well with others." Early socialization and exposure help ensure their ease with other dogs. However, if food is involved, all bets are off. Even with their overall friendliness, owning two intact or same-age males may not be a good idea.

LOW TERRITORIAL AGGRESSION

Though there are cases where Basset Hounds have come to the aid of their owners, it isn't normal behavior for them. Scent hounds will let you know someone is at the door; afterwards the person is your problem. Normally, hounds are friendly to strangers.

COMMON PROBLEMS – Housebreaking, howling, running off, garbage eating, possessive and defensive aggression.

GOOD HOMES – People who have access to fenced-in areas or time for long walks on-lead. If you enjoy a happy, sweet dog with a hobby—his nose—you'll love scent hounds. Early training and socialization are important. If you want instant, doting obedience, look elsewhere. Strive for a rock-solid "Come," but don't bet his life on it by allowing him unfenced freedom. Expect to use a crate for well over a year. Investing in lidded trash cans is money well spent. Expect to tend ears, and sometimes eyes, on a regular basis.

Sighthounds:
Greyhound, Afghan, Irish Wolfhound, Whippet, Borzoi

SUZANNAH VALENTINETTI

Sighthounds chase down game. Once they are released, they take off like a shot. Nothing can tear their eyes off their prize. When the game is caught, they do not retrieve it; instead, the owner must come to the dog. Sighthounds are some of the most ancient breeds of record; they lived closely with their human companions, often highly prized and carefully cared for.

VISUALLY STIMULATED

Suddenly a sighthound's head snaps up and he is scanning something on the horizon. If it moves, a sighthound will watch it. If he can, he may well give chase. The good news is that often when the object disappears from sight, it also disappears from mind.

RUNNING-RELATED DEAFNESS

A sighthound usually comes back in his own good time and normally in a huge circle. When they are in hot pursuit, few will listen. If you want proof of this, go to just about any lure coursing event (where sighthounds race after mechanical prey) and watch owners trying to retrieve their dogs.

COMFORT SEEKING

In most cases, low body fat and little coat means they have no padding or fur. Who can blame them for seeking out a soft sleeping spot? They will sleep on your furniture and bed; arguing about that will only lead to frustration on both sides. Toss a sheet over an old chair and make it theirs.

SENSITIVE

Emotionally? Physically? Mentally? Yes to all of the above. Speak harshly to an Irish Wolfhound and she may be in despair for hours. When Brian reacted with loud surprise after our Deerhound, Piper, hopped onto him while he was napping (Piper did not see him underneath the thick down comforter), Piper was traumatized. For months—literally, months—he would not even walk down the hall to our bedroom.

Such a reaction is quite typical. A retriever would have flung himself on Brian, licking his face; and a sighthound decides the whole room is mined. Daily handling from puppyhood is an excellent idea. Make surprises a game. Teach him what you want him to do if he is startled. Don't use a lot of force on these dogs; it is neither justified nor useful. These simple things can go a long way to making his life, and yours, easier.

COMMON PROBLEMS – Not coming when called, destructiveness, defensive aggression, chasing animals.

GOOD HOMES – People who appreciate the beauty of these animals, have access to fenced areas, and don't mind the dog on the furniture will love sighthounds. These are not the dogs for tricks, retrieving, or protection. They are wonderful dogs to love and cherish. With the right methods and attitude, they are absolutely trainable.

In the exercise department, the good news is that sighthounds don't have a ton of endurance; they are built for bursts of brilliant speed rather than daylong marathons. A few moderate walks and a half-hour run every day, or even every other day once a sighthound is mature, are all that is usually required.

Property Guards:
Doberman Pinscher, Rottweiler, Boxer, Great Dane, Giant Schnauzer

Back when humans huddled around the campfire, one of the first things dogs did for us was alert us to intruders. This early warning system has been valued by countless generations of humans.

As our societies developed and we acquired more and more stuff to protect, we wanted more and more help protecting it. Property guards, alert, physically powerful, mentally assertive, who would react to threats with aggression if necessary, were developed.

While these traits may sound terrific, most of these guard dogs are not for the casual owner. They need careful management, daily training, constant supervision, and knowledgeable rearing. Softer, less aggressive, and easier to manage than some of their counterparts are Boxers, Great Danes, and Dobermans. They may still be a challenge for some, but they are generally easier to own than the more assertive Rottweiler or Giant Schnauzer.

SARAH WILSON

AGGRESSION—ALL KINDS

Since aggression is their heritage and their purpose, it should come as no surprise that aggression can be their problem. Take any sign of aggression seriously and get immediate help.

Keep in mind that these dogs were bred to respond to threats with aggression. Do not use violence or anger in your training, or you may meet that heritage head-on. If you do, you caused it. Don't blame the dog.

STRONG-MINDED AND SURE OF THEMSELVES

These dogs will give you their soul if they respect you. Respect is earned through firm, consistent leadership, not with harsh words or actions. These breeds can be quite difficult to reach mentally once they are focused on something. You must be equally focused and determined to own one successfully. If you don't like to force your will calmly on another living thing, avoid this group. If you understand that as the leader, it is your job to call the shots in a relaxed but non-negotiable way, consider one—maybe. We recommend a female, because in these breeds they are generally less assertive.

TAKE ACTION INTO THEIR OWN HANDS

Don't expect a Giant Schnauzer to wait for you to tell him what to do. He'll know what needs doing and will do it! That is normal for the breed; not always desirable, but normal. Excellent verbal control, the kind that needs daily work to maintain, is mandatory.

BARKING

These dogs bark. When they're behind a fence, they can bark a lot. Their history directs them to keep everything and everyone away from their turf. If you want a dog you can leave outside for a few hours and have peace and quiet, this group is not the place to look.

POWERFUL

Created to be intimidating, these animals are. We've seen more than one owner who bought the dog hoping to intimidate others end up being intimidated himself.

Early training at puppy class and daily handling exercises can help you and your puppy develop understanding and mutual respect. If at any time you are the least bit frightened of your dog, get professional help immediately. If a powerful guard breed suspects he has cowed you, you are in serious trouble.

COMMON PROBLEMS – Overprotectiveness, barking, jumping, chewing, possessiveness, fighting with other dogs, dominance and territorial aggression, biting out of fear.

GOOD HOMES – Experienced dog owners with the time for the exercise, intensive training, and socialization required. Early exposure to all kinds of people and

Neutering

Many people—read here: "most men"—have a strong response to the concept of neutering, a response that normally begins with crossing their legs.

Please, gentlemen, we're not talking about you here. Try thinking of it this way: Few people who ride horses ride stallions. Why? Because they are too powerful, strong-willed, and assertive, which means they are harder to control and less predictable than geldings.

Would you let your children handle a stallion? How about walk into a field with a bull? Dogs are animals, not people. Neutering them will make them calmer, better pets, less prone to biting, wandering, fighting with other dogs, and leg lifting.

If the practice still bothers you, take heart. There is even a company that makes fake testicles for dogs. Take the real ones out, put the fake ones in.

You can have your cake and eat it too, so to speak.

animals is mandatory. Owner must be calm, consistent, positive, and knowledgeable. Training is necessary for the life of the dog.

All male pets of these breeds should be neutered as soon as possible, no later than six months of age. Why? Because the most frequent biters are unneutered males.

Draft/Rescue Dogs:
Newfoundland, Saint Bernard, Bernese Mountain Dog

Whether bred to pull carts to market or haul drowning people out of the waves, these breeds have a strong and inherent devotion to humans. These dogs worked closely for and with people. They had to be powerful to do their jobs well, hence their large size. How does this heritage influence them?

GENTLE

Normally, these dogs are some of the sweetest around. Laid-back, easygoing, and eager to please, they make wonderful companions for people who don't mind hair on the walls and drool on the floor.

POWERFUL

Because they range from big to mammoth, you must have verbal control over these dogs. Start training no later than three months old, and stick with it. Even if their intentions are good, they can knock over an adult like a bowling pin.

MARIAN ADAMS

TRAINABLE

Bred to work with humans, these dogs want to please us. This makes training fun for both you and your dog. They are adaptable to most methods, so keep in mind our favorite adage—"fun, fair, firm"—then go, go, go! Few things are more impressive than a massive dog under excellent verbal control.

COMMON PROBLEMS – Shyness, pulling on lead, jumping.

GOOD HOMES – These dogs are recommended for concerned owners who have time each day to train and exercise their pet, owners with a large car and enough room and enough money to care properly for these often immense animals. Fastidious housekeepers look elsewhere.

CAUTION – Both Bernese Mountain Dogs and Saint Bernards have some aggression and shyness problems in their ranks, and all of the giants have orthopedic problems to worry about. Research your breed and pup carefully if you decide to own one of these great dogs.

Sled Dogs:
Siberian Husky, Alaskan Malamute, Samoyed

Bred for transportation in snowbound areas, most were multipurpose dogs that also helped with hunting and/or herding. Powerful animals that love to pull, these dogs worked with other dogs. Though often harnessed to a sled, these dogs are not known for their instant obedience. Living in the northern wilds created dogs with lots of hair, endurance, energy, and a heck of a voice — after all, there were no neighbors around to complain.

SARAH WILSON

ATHLETES
These guys can run and run and run. A lot of training needs to happen before they can be trusted off-leash — if they ever can be trusted. Expect to spend more than an hour a day outside, especially during the first couple of years. If a sled dog is bored or restless and has unsupervised access to your stuff, chewing can be a problem. Using a crate is an excellent preventative measure.

INDEPENDENT
They think for themselves and act on their own best instincts. This is another trait that renders a lead mandatory! Loving but not doting, these are interesting and entertaining companions for people who want to be loved but not fawned over.

DIGGERS
The instincts in these breeds are close to the surface. They know how to take care of themselves. Digging a shallow pit under a shady bush is a great way to stay cool. Few of these dogs can resist such a sensible approach to comfort.

Wolf Hybrids

There are people out there who will make money selling you anything, including wolf hybrids (wolf-dog crosses). These are not pets but dangerous animals that do not behave like dogs. Wolves are wonderful—when they're running free in Yellowstone Park. They were never intended to live in your home. Wolves are actually shy animals who would rather flee than fight. When you mix dogs and wolves you take the useful "run away" and "fear of humans" instincts out of the wolf and add independence, instability, and primitive behaviors to the dog. What you get is 100 percent bad news.

HOWLERS AND "TALKERS"

Expect to hear a happy "Ouuuooo" when your dog greets you. If left alone, they may well howl. Most are not especially barky.

PREDATORY

Hunter's blood courses through their veins and many will chase after, and some will dispatch, smaller animals if allowed to. They can usually be taught to respect other pets in the house, but not always outside.

COMMON PROBLEMS – Digging, destructive chewing, howling, housebreaking, fighting with other dogs, Olympic-scale leash pulling, predatory behavior, running off.

GOOD HOMES – Easygoing, active people who want an athletic, fun companion who doesn't hang on their every word. Great for joggers and hikers. People who enjoy bright dogs with a wicked sense of humor should enjoy this group. If you can't bring yourself to use a crate, don't get a sled dog. You must be tolerant of hair in vast quantities during the twice-a-year shedding periods.

Toys:
Pug, Papillon, Maltese, Yorkshire Terrier

When human societies were developed enough to have an upper class, they had developed enough to give some lucky folks some free time. The bored rich wanted companions; not rough-and-tumble companions, but sweet, adorable, charming companions. That is how many toys came into being—as entertainment for royalty. Other toys are scaled-down versions of larger breeds. They all have one thing in common: They were created for companionship. Small they are, playthings they are not. These are some of the most intelligent, strong-minded, and creative dogs around. Never underestimate them.

EASILY SPOILED

Because of their size and their purpose (amusing us), toys lend themselves to fabulous amounts of spoiling. They are often doted on, allowed to run wild, and permitted to do pretty much as they please. This indulgence can lead to aggression, leg lifting, fearfulness, shyness, and general neurosis. Do your toy a favor and treat him like a dog.

CHRISTINE M. PELLICANO

HOUSEBREAKING CHALLENGES

A dog likes to keep his "home" area clean. The problem for toys is that your kitchen feels more like a football stadium than a cozy den (as it might for a larger dog). That proportional largeness makes it easy for them to think that one area is okay to use as a toilet because there is still plenty of room left to live in.

This proportional perspective applies to us, but in different ways. While it is immediately clear that a Saint Bernard pile in the house is a problem, a tiny little Maltese dropping may not seem like much of a bother. Housebreaking is not difficult to achieve. We list plenty of excellent training resources in the back of this book. All you need for success is information and commitment.

SMART

There is no stupid toy. Interactive, demanding, endearing, infuriating, these dogs are never boring. If you are not ready for a dog to become an integral part of your life, do not get a toy. They will settle for nothing less than being your best friend, most trusted confidant, fearless protector, favorite lap warmer, and, oh yes, bathroom pal, too, because you're never going there alone again.

BAD ATTITUDE

This comes from the spoiling, not from the dog. But endless cooing, stroking, and babying would bring out the worst in any of us. If you want to avoid aggression, leg lifting, and general brattiness, hold your bright little toy to a high standard of behavior, not to your breast.

COMMON PROBLEMS – Housebreaking, aggression, leg lifting, barking, hyperactivity, finicky eating, shyness, and other owner-supported problems.

GOOD HOMES – Adults and older, careful children with time for daily play, training, and grooming. Homebodies are fine. If you stick the pup in your shoulder bag when you do errands, he'll get socialized in no time. Owner must be firm and consistent in the face of extreme cuteness. No babying allowed!

Herding Dogs:
Collie, German Shepherd Dog, Shetland Sheepdog, Border Collie, Australian Shepherd

Created to work closely with people, think independently when necessary, work long hours, and control large moving things, herding breeds are smart problem-solvers. Certain breeds bark to move their charges.

These dogs need work; if you don't supply it they will make their own. Eager to learn, they are usually a joy to train. They can also be overprotective of house and family.

Individuals of these breeds can have severe shyness problems and sensitivity to noises. All need intensive, early socialization and training to grow up to be stable, predictable companions.

CHASING BEHAVIORS

Expect and correct car chasing, bicycle hounding, and the like from these movement-stimulated breeds.

MOVEMENT-STIMULATED NIPPING

Predictably, many of these dogs nip at the heels of humans the way they nip at the heels of livestock. Running children who emit high-pitched sounds can be favorite targets. This behavior is controllable through training and sensible management.

TONI KAY

UNWANTED ACTIVITY

Pacing, spinning, and circling are all normal behaviors if your herding dog is under-exercised, and sometimes even when he is adequately exercised. These dogs have the desire and the endurance to work all day. You must exercise them mentally with training and physically with activity—every day. Rain or shine, sleet or snow, these dogs need to work!

BARKING

Several of these breeds (Shelties, Pulik, and Beardies spring to mind) use their bark when they work livestock. Because this was a desirable trait, these dogs still tend to bark when excited, eager, happy, or frustrated. Training may give you some control over barking, but it is doubtful you will ever control it completely.

HIGHLY TRAINABLE

These breeds worked closely with humans; consequently, all are highly intelligent. Some people do not realize that a well-trained herding dog responds instantly to a command but does it in a way that makes sense in that situation. A herding dog will execute a command to "Come bye" (go clockwise around the flock) one way if he is rounding up a small flock of frightened sheep, and another way if he is working with a large herd of feisty young cattle. The dog will still go clockwise, but he will do so faster or slower, closer or farther away, depending on what he thinks will work best with those animals. He thinks—so he may interpret your commands. They learn quickly and retain information well, but persistent training is necessary to get decent verbal control over these dogs.

COMMON PROBLEMS – Shyness, overprotectiveness, barking, hyperactivity, sound sensitivity, car chasing, dominance and territorial aggression, fighting with other dogs.

GOOD HOMES – Active, calm people with the time for exercise, training, and intensive socialization. A fenced yard is a must. Owner must enjoy training, be decisive, consistent, and persistent.

Non-Sporting/Rare

Non-Sporting is a catchall group. Each breed must be judged by the purpose for which it was created; no generalities can be drawn. Some of the most popular and challenging breeds fall into these ranks—Chow, Dalmatian, Lhasa Apso, and Chinese Shar Pei—so be sure to do your homework carefully. The same instructions hold true for rare breeds.

SARAH WILSON

There are always a few rare breeds in popularity. Proceed with caution! Many of these up-and-coming breeds are hunting or guard dogs. Do you really want a dog around who was created to—and whose parents loved to—kill bears? Do you have a bear problem? Black bear in your basement? Grizzlies in your garage?

What's a "Poo"?

Cock-a-Poo? Yorkie-Poo? Mix anything with a Poodle and you get a Something-Poo. While they may make fabulous pets—we've known several that we liked a lot—they are not purebreds and should not be sold in stores for hundreds of dollars a puppy. Don't pay through the nose for a mutt with a fancy name.

If you do not have a bear problem then you do not need this breed. Choose a family companion to do what you need him to do every day of his long life: love your kids and chase a tennis ball.

Large, powerful breeds naively bought for some perceived protection end up injuring family members—often the children—much more frequently than they save lives.

Understanding the Breed Chapters

These chapters arc

> for people who want to know which breeds might fit their lifestyle or needs.

> for people wise enough to realize that while looks count, they are not the sole or even primary reason to select a breed.

> two people's experience. This is not gospel, nor is it written in stone. This is just our opinion. Some people will agree, some will not. That's an inevitable outcome of having opinions

These chapters are not

> a review of every breed. They are a review of some of our favorite breeds for

LARRY G. LOVIG

> these situations. We elected not to review any breed we had not worked with in sufficient numbers to form an opinion or was so rare that finding one might be really difficult. Several breeds were also excluded because, as our mothers taught us, "If you don't have anything nice to say . . ." If you don't like our silence, take it up with our moms.

> an unbiased look. Every breed has its pluses and minuses, which we have tried to include here. We think informed owners make the best owners.

> funded by any clubs or vested interest groups. We don't have to please anyone but ourselves.

Each breed is assessed in a series of ways. Here are a few things you should know about these categories.

USUAL PLUSES

Here are the classic breed traits as we know them. Some say you can't generalize about breed behavior. Of course you can. Breeds were developed to perform certain tasks, and those tasks gave rise to behavioral and temperamental characteristics. You can't say that every individual in a breed has those characteristics. There is wide variation in all dog breeds, but those exceptions do not disprove the rule.

POSSIBLE DRAWBACKS

The nature of a drawback (or a plus, for that matter) is personal. If someone lives in a desolate cabin, having a dog that is suspicious of strangers would hardly be a problem; it might even be a boon. A busy household full of children might find that same dog endlessly trying. A sedate city-dweller might find a dog's high activity level troublesome, while a suburban jogger might enjoy it. "Possible Drawbacks" lists things *we* consider drawbacks; you'll have to decide for yourself.

HEIGHT AND WEIGHT

What the breed standard calls for and what actually exists in people's homes are completely different. A Golden Retriever "ought" to be around sixty pounds, but we've met several that were over ninety-five. Ask what size the parents are; that should give you some idea of the dimensions your pup will mature into.

Please do not get hung up on size. You will be narrowing your options for a completely aesthetic reason. An eighty-pound German Shepherd Dog is just as fine a companion as a Shepherd that weighs 110 pounds and is less prone to certain health problems.

COLOR

This is the inexperienced dog person's downfall. Take our word for it: Finding a healthy, mentally stable dog is challenging enough, and if you limit your options with color, you may end up making the wrong choice for the worst reasons.

A blue merle Australian Shepherd puppy
SARAH WILSON

When Sarah went hunting for her first Australian Shepherd, she wanted a blue merle female. Blue merle is a mix of gray, white, and black. She got a black male who is one of the world's great dogs. She would not trade him for anything. Thank goodness she didn't skip over him for something as silly as sex or coat color. Now

The Meaning of "Merle"

"Merle" is a color pattern, a patchwork. There is blue merle—a combination of black, gray, and white—and red merle, a combination of dark red, light red, and white.

"Merle" can mean "dangerous." If two merles are bred together, chances are good that some puppies will be born deaf, retarded, or otherwise handicapped. Such defects are not always easy to see at seven or eight weeks of age. Either avoid pups from such crosses, or have the pup checked over immediately for such defects by your veterinarian.

Sarah thinks black is the prettiest color. Love changes things. It will change things for you, too.

GROOMING

Isn't that little Maltese elegant with his flowing locks? Wouldn't a dog like that be wonderful around the house? Well, dogs like that don't wander around the house. For the most part they sit in wire cages, with their hair oiled and rolled up in paper, looking for all the world like some 1950s mother caught in curlers. They don't play in the grass, they don't romp with other dogs; they might muss their hair.

These lovely dog pictures are like photographs of *Sports Illustrated* swimsuit models—yup, gorgeous, but not a reflection of reality. Keep long-coated dogs in a shorter clip; it will make life easier for both of you.

SHEDDING

Dogs have hair, and that hair, usually, falls out at some point. Regular brushing and a good diet help lessen shedding, as do some nutritional supplements, but nothing stops it altogether. Shedding is a natural phenomenon. It comes with the dog-owning territory. If shedding is really unappealing to you, look in "The Low-Shed Breeds" for suggestions.

TRAINING

Training is our bread and butter, so it comes as no surprise that we consider this mandatory. Communication brings clarity to your dog's world. Clarity brings calmness. Calmness brings sanity to both your worlds. Sanity is a blessing. Thus, training is a blessing.

There are a confusing number of methods out there, which people seem to follow with nearly religious zeal. There are people who use only food rewards to teach the dog and others who consider that bribery. Some people think training collars are cruel, while others use them with great success.

Find one method that you like and that works. It does no good to like a method if you make no progress with your dog, nor does it help if the dog complies with your commands but you hate the way you made him obey. Have faith; there are other ways. Those of us in the field collect methods like favorite recipes—there will almost always be a use.

EXERCISE

One of the prime reasons dogs develop problem behaviors is lack of adequate exercise. What a certain breed needs, and what an individual within a breed needs, will vary, but certain generalizations can be made. Young dogs need more running time than older dogs. Really young dogs, especially of the larger breeds, need protection from overexertion and injury, so discuss the best exercise program with your breeder and veterinarian before you begin.

CHILDREN

A dog is your child's companion, not his plaything. A dog can be a playmate given the right dog, the right kid, and proper parental supervision.

Teach your child to respect your dog, just as you demand that she respect other children. If the dog gets up and moves away during play, your child must not follow. The dog has just stated that he has had enough. If you allow the child to chase after the dog, you are setting up your child for a bite.

Saying "I can't control my kid" is not acceptable. No doubt you have managed to keep your child from kicking babies or spitting on strangers. Take the same stance with behavior toward the dog.

In most cases, it is easier on you, the child, and the dog if you wait until your child is older to add a canine companion. Older usually means five or six, but you are the best judge of your child's personality. If your child is naturally gentle and calm, a bit younger may well be appropriate. If "impulsive," "active," and "physical" better describe your child, why not wait a little longer?

CHRISTINE M. PELLICANO

OTHER PETS

If you are adding a dog to your cat-ruled house, make sure your cat has several safe havens to retreat to when you introduce the new dog. Setting up baby gates so the cat can flee easily to safety will keep peace in your household. It can take a cat weeks, or longer, to adjust to a new dog.

When you add a second dog to a household, it's best to add the opposite sex. If you already have two dogs, add the opposite sex of your dominant dog. Keeping two or more years between the ages of your dogs also helps reduce tension. Neutering males at a young age can prevent aggression from developing, making life easier for all concerned.

BITE POTENTIAL

Bite potential varies widely from breed to breed, as well as within each breed. Potential is no guarantee. Even the sweetest breed can harbor a biter and even the sweetest dog can bite given the right circumstances. The ratings here are guidelines, not promises.

Our general ratings refer to a stable, sound specimen that has been raised, socialized, and trained appropriately. He lives in a sane home where he isn't hurt, harassed, or endlessly indulged. Giving an animal everything he wants the moment he wants it has probably created more aggression in dogs than anything else has.

POSSIBLE HEALTH CONCERNS

Some common health concerns specific to each breed are listed here. Occasionally a rare risk may have sneaked into our listings, as resources often do not note the percentages of affected dogs in any breed. You should definitely ask breeders for more detailed information.

SPECIAL COMMENTS

This is a catchall area for specialized health, management, rearing, or selection issues.

ALSO SUITED FOR

Dogs listed here can be grouped under more than one heading. Many of these fine breeds are multitalented dogs. Utilize these lists to maximize your options in selecting a dog that is right for you.

Good Dogs That Are Hard to Find

In this category you find some of the most wonderful breeds in the canine world. So wonderful, in fact, that they are extremely popular. Popularity is no favor to any breed of dog, as some people will breed unstable dogs to unhealthy dogs just to get those precious, income-generating pups.

In every breed, ethical breeders struggle against this riptide, but the sheer numbers of animals produced per year puts these ethical breeders in the minority. Thus, finding a healthy, stable dog from the most popular breeds is a challenge. Proceed with great caution. Take your time; visit puppies without checks or cash in your pockets. Walk away and think about your decision. Reread the section on finding a good breeder. Keep chanting to yourself: "All puppies are cute, all puppies are cute, all puppies . . ."

DIANE LARATTA

American Cocker Spaniel

USUAL PLUSES

These little gems have been popular for decades, and those decades have turned many of these diamonds into cubic zirconia. At their best, they are delightful, happy companions that love everyone with equal enthusiasm. Sweet and easy to train, they deserve the adulation they have accrued.

POSSIBLE DRAWBACKS

In our years, we have trained several hundred American Cocker Spaniels, and we can recall only a handful of wonderful ones. The rest were poorly bred specimens, prone to unwanted behavior that ran the gamut from really annoying, chronic submissive wetting to downright horrendous aggression.

Overbreeding has compromised the health of these dogs. Chronic ear infections and skin and eye problems are almost routine. We know Cockers that had to have ear canals surgically removed as the only answer to ongoing infections. Do *not* buy a Cocker from a pet store.

HEIGHT
14–15 inches.

WEIGHT
Under 28 pounds.

COLOR

Most commonly buff or black. Other colors are parti (meaning white plus another color), chocolate, black and tan, red, or silver. Though any color Cocker can be good or bad, we've met more than our fair share of troubled buff-colored males.

GROOMING

Professional assistance is mandatory. Cockers have a wide range of coat, but in a well-bred Cocker you will have to get him groomed every eight weeks or so. At-home brushing and ear maintenance is essential.

SHEDDING
Moderate.

TRAINING

Suggested. With a good Cocker, it will be fun. With an unstable Cocker, it is mandatory, though it will not always be the total answer to your problems.

EXERCISE

Recommended. Young dogs need daily romps to let off steam productively, but as breeds go, their energy level is manageable.

CHILDREN

Assuming it's a good Cocker, fine.

LAURA WOLFF

OTHER PETS

Assuming it's a good Cocker, fine.

BITE POTENTIAL

Low to virtually none in a well-bred, well-reared, well-socialized dog, but downright inevitable in an unstable one.

POSSIBLE HEALTH CONCERNS

Hip dysplasia (HD), progressive retinal atrophy (PRA), cataracts, disk disease, subluxating patellas, Legg-Calves Perthes disease, Factor X deficiency, and glaucoma, to name a few. The long list even includes things as bizarre as reverse rear legs, which are exactly what they sound like.

SPECIAL COMMENTS

Lady and the Tramp was a cartoon. Visit real American Cocker Spaniels before you elect to spend your life with one.

ALSO SUITED FOR

City Dog.

Beagle

USUAL PLUSES

Beagle fans point out their good looks, adaptable nature, and sweet disposition. These fine traits, and the fact that they are so darn cute, have kept them in the top ten favorite breeds for many years. Possessing great curiosity and no small measure of problem-solving ability, Beagles are entertaining companions.

POSSIBLE DRAWBACKS

In our experience, these are not always easy dogs to own. No Beagle we know has ever said no to his nose. This gift (and obsession) makes them prone to chronic food stealing, garbage raiding, and wandering. Beagles can be noisy. Howling when alone is not uncommon. Housebreaking may be a challenge. Avoid shyness and timidity through careful selection and sensible rearing. Last, though not normally aggressive, when they are they are quite nasty.

HEIGHT

Two sizes: 10–13 inches and 13–15 inches.

WEIGHT

13-incher: 18–20 pounds; 15-incher: 20–30 pounds.

COLOR

White, black, and/or tan.

GROOMING

Minimal coat care. Regular ear care required.

SHEDDING

Moderate.

TRAINING

Mandatory, as Beagles are independent-minded. Early and regular training is the best way to instill words like "Come," "Out," and "Leave it." Food works extremely well as a Beagle motivator. Keep him on-lead or inside a fence; he will give chase if he has the opportunity.

EXERCISE

Mandatory. Because they are prone to being overweight when they get older and mischievously active when young, exercise for the life of your dog is important. Long walks twice a day are a good start.

CHILDREN

The good ones are good with children. Beagles do not usually enjoy ear pulling, contrary to President Johnson's famous photo. Unstable, shy, or overly assertive Beagles are not good companions for anyone.

JACK SHORF

OTHER PETS

Usually fine.

BITE POTENTIAL

Low to high. Select carefully.

POSSIBLE HEALTH CONCERNS

Generally long-lived, Beagles can suffer from eye, heart, back, kidney, and skin problems.

SPECIAL COMMENTS

Avoid field-bred lines if you want an indoor companion. Obesity plagues these dogs, so watch food intake and exercise closely. So-called Pocket Beagles, miniature hereditary nightmares, should be avoided.

ALSO SUITED FOR

Watchdog.

Doberman Pinscher

USUAL PLUSES

Loyal to their family, energetic, athletic dogs that would rather steal one end of the couch than cause trouble. Despite their rough reputation and fierce looks, Dobes are generally sweet, soft dogs.

POSSIBLE DRAWBACKS

Dobermans went through a nasty population boom a couple of decades back, which left them with the usual genetic flotsam and jetsam. Temperaments vary from cowardly to aggressive. Most breeders are working hard to improve their breed constantly, but quiz them carefully on temperament. We've heard experienced breeders claim that their dogs bite because the animals "know you are being silly. They are just correcting you. My dogs correct my husband for being silly all the time." Yikes!

HEIGHT

24–28 inches.
Some much larger.

WEIGHT

60–85 pounds, although I know a
seven-month-old pup that is 96 pounds!

COLOR

Black and tan, red and tan are the most common and have fewer problems than the less common colors like blue, white, and fawn (Isabella). "Fewer problems" is a relative term, as Dobies have many serious health and temperament issues.

BRUCE DAVID KUREK

GROOMING

Minimal.

SHEDDING

Minimal.

TRAINING

Professional assistance mandatory. These dogs have a reputation for being aggressive. What would be "no big deal" with another breed may be perceived as a major problem with a Doberman. Start training and socializing your dog immediately. Find a good training school and go nonstop for the first eighteen months. Do not use, and do not allow anyone else to use, harsh physical corrections. This kind of abusive handling can cause aggression in Dobes.

EXERCISE

Mandatory. A Doberman running full-out is a thing of beauty. They have a grace and symmetry that few dogs outside the sighthound group possess. They need an hour or more of exercise a day, especially during the first few years.

CHILDREN

Okay with older children, but this varies. Calm dogs are marvelous with almost any age person, but a high-strung, snappish Dobie should not be anywhere near a child.

OTHER PETS

Careful! Male Dobes are notorious for their aggression toward other males. Do not mix assertive males with dogs of the same age, sex, or of much smaller size without careful consideration.

BITE POTENTIAL

Low to high.

POSSIBLE HEALTH CONCERNS

Lots, sadly. Hip dysplasia, von Willebrand's disease, bloat, cancer, heart disease, auto-immune problems, skin problems, thyroid and liver disorders.

SPECIAL COMMENTS

If you want a tough, macho dog, skip over the Doberman. If you want a sweet dog that looks like a tough, macho dog, this breed may be perfect for you.

ALSO SUITED FOR

Watchdog.

Protection Training? *No!*

The best canine protection a pet home can have is a well-trained dog who is constantly at your side. No pet dog should be protection-trained. The moment he is, he is no longer a pet.

Your home liability insurance can be negated if you attack- or protection-train your dog. You know your dog can and will bite: If your dog ever bites anyone, for any reason, you will have little legal protection. Furthermore, if you can't control your dog's jumping on guests, what makes you think you will be able to control him when he is aggressive? You will never be able to completely relax with your dog again. You will always have to think: Where is he? What is he doing? Who is interacting with him?

We could make a great deal of money protection-training dogs, but we never do it. Why? Because it puts both the people and the dogs we love at risk.

English Springer Spaniel

USUAL PLUSES

Gregarious, warm, sweet-tempered dog with a happy outlook on the world. To a nice Springer there are no strangers, simply friends he hasn't yet met. A delightful, mid-sized companion that, when exercised properly and trained, fits easily into many families.

POSSIBLE DRAWBACKS

Aggression haunts the halls of the Springer breed. Scary aggression, turn-on-you-in-a-second aggression that even the most experienced trainer approaches with caution. This problem is seen mostly in males. Serious breeders are working hard to correct this problem and, happily, have made some headway in the last few years.

Other problems such as dominance, possessiveness, and shyness are also found. Without appropriate exercise and training, Springers can be chewers, diggers, barkers, and jumpers.

HEIGHT
19–20 inches.

WEIGHT
About 40–55 pounds.

SARAH WILSON

COLOR
Black or liver and white, roan, or tricolor. The latter two are much less common than the first two.

GROOMING
Moderate to a lot. Professional care recommended every ten to twelve weeks for heavily coated dogs.

SHEDDING
Moderate.

TRAINING
Recommended. With males, mandatory! You'll never regret teaching your dog both his place and yours in his life. The more assertive the dog, the more daily training is required.

EXERCISE

Mandatory. They need rigorous runs every day. A fenced-in area and another playful dog will help your dog burn off excess energy in a positive way.

CHILDREN

A good Springer is a joy with children. May be a bit too bouncy at times, but a sweet, well-meaning tail wagger. An aggressive Springer is not safe with adults, never mind children.

OTHER PETS

Usually terrific, but with the same concerns as above.

BITE POTENTIAL

Low to high.

POSSIBLE HEALTH CONCERNS

Hip dysplasia, allergies, chronic ear problems, seizures, blood and heart disorders. Insist on both eye and hip certification. Neuter males as early as your veterinarian will do it—no later than 6 months of age.

ALICE RENDALL

SPECIAL COMMENTS

Field-bred Springers (bred strictly for hunting) are smaller, more wiry dogs with shorter hair, more white color, and much more energy than the show line dogs. Sarah had one for a few years. Running Sasha several hours a day was not simply a good idea, it was not optional. Even with an hour of running a day, Sasha chewed her feet and ran circles in the house. For a companion, look for a multipurpose show line that is involved in several canine activities.

ALSO SUITED FOR

High-Input, High-Output Dog.

German Shepherd Dog

USUAL PLUSES

If any breed is renowned for its versatility, it is this one. Rin Tin Tin created this image years ago, and the breed lives up to that reputation every day. They find the lost, guide the blind, herd the sheep, apprehend the bad guy, protect our police officers, watch over our homes, warm our feet, and accompany us on every adventure. There are few things a good German Shepherd Dog cannot do.

POSSIBLE DRAWBACKS

We love these dogs dearly, but boy is the Shepherd breed full of neurotic, sickly, unsound, aggressive, shy dogs. Long one of the most popular dogs in the world, GSDs have widespread genetic and temperament problems. Because they bond so strongly with their people, overattachment, separation anxiety, fearfulness of new situations, and overprotectiveness can develop.

HEIGHT

22–26 inches.
Some are much bigger.

WEIGHT

65–100 pounds.
Again, some are much larger.

COLOR

Black and tan, solid black, sable (gray), or white. Whites are not showable under the AKC standard but are still purebred Shepherds.

GROOMING

Generally, a good brushing once a week will do. During shedding, brush every day and prepare to be amazed. Long-coated Shepherds require more care.

SHEDDING

The GSD is a double-coated breed, and double-coated breeds shed. Sometime in the spring and the fall, your dog will shed, and when he does, you will not believe the amount of hair that comes out. You will be brushing daily, getting enough hair to build several small dogs, and still the dog will shed. This lasts a couple of weeks.

TRAINING

Professional assistance mandatory. Start in puppy kindergarten and continue for the first two years. Train, socialize, then train some more. Do not reward cowardice or aggression. Try not to reward whining, as many become annoyingly vocal. Males should be neutered early.

EXERCISE

Mandatory. Exercise needs vary widely, but most GSDs need at least two major play/exercise sessions a day to be reasonable. Some of the hyper ones are a bottom-less pit in this department.

CHILDREN

Varies. Some are excellent, some dangerous.

OTHER PETS

Varies. Our cats accompany us on walks with our Shep-herds. Other Shepherds try to kill cats on sight. Some of this behavior is inherited predatory drive, some of it is rearing and general lack of control.

BITE POTENTIAL

Moderate to high. These are smart, assertive dogs that need training and sensible management. A neurotic dog will never be reliable in the average home.

JOAN WEBB

POSSIBLE HEALTH CONCERNS

Are you ready? Orthopedic problems: hip dysplasia, elbow dysplasia, spinal degeneration, development problems: You name it, it's here. Auto-immune disease, subaortic stenosis (SAS), thyroid dysfunction, skin disorders, and serious gastrointestinal problems are all too common. Poor temperament is so com-mon that a stable, confident, calm Shepherd is a surprise to many.

SPECIAL COMMENTS

A good GSD offers intelligence and devotion that is hard to match; a poor specimen offers heartbreak for all concerned. The unhealthy, unstable dogs far outweigh the wonderful, stalwart companions we are all hoping to find when we invite one of these dogs into our homes.

ALSO SUITED FOR

Watchdog, Not for Everyone.

Golden Retriever

USUAL PLUSES

Who can imagine a sweeter dog than the Golden? The poster pet endorsing the family dog: "Good with children" is assumed. Loving, goofy, devoted to the point of fawning, these are simply some of the nicest dogs we humans ever managed to breed.

POSSIBLE DRAWBACKS

The decline of this fine breed brings us much sadness. Now all too many are short-lived, problem-prone, and temperamentally weak. More than a few are truly pig-headed. We never used to see any aggression and now see dog aggression, dominance aggression, territorial aggression . . . you get the picture.

On the opposite end of the scale, we find the fearful, groveling, submissive-wetting Golden. A good specimen is an incredible family/all-round dog; just be prepared to search, beg, and wait for the right animal. It is well worth the effort.

HEIGHT
21½–24 inches.

WEIGHT
55–75 pounds.

COLOR

From the palest cream to the darkest red. Popular colors are influenced by showring fads. Of the dogs we see, the darkest reds have field blood in their veins, which may make them more active than the average family had in mind.

GROOMING

Minimal to a lot. Coat amount and quality varies. The more show dog there is in your dog, the more grooming will be required.

SHEDDING

Moderate to a lot.

TRAINING

Mandatory. These are exuberant, physical, powerful dogs that will drag you down the street if you don't teach them otherwise. Highly trainable; the top AKC obedience dogs in the United States are almost exclusively Goldens.

EXERCISE

Mandatory, especially during the first three years. Puppy kindergarten and a good crate will get you off on the right foot.

CHILDREN

Made for each other—if you have a good Golden and if you supervise your children. Sins of enthusiasm like mouthing, knocking kids down, and too much licking are common if the dog is untrained.

OTHER PETS

Good—*if* you have a good Golden.

BITE POTENTIAL

Low to, sadly, high; range matches good specimen to bad.

POSSIBLE HEALTH CONCERNS

Subaortic stenosis (SAS), bloat, cancer, hip dysplasia, elbow dysplasia, progressive retinal atrophy, panosteitis, juvenile cataracts, epilepsy, flea allergy.

SPECIAL COMMENTS

Field-bred Goldens as well as some top obedience lines (both of which are usually more wiry and a darker red than show stock) can have an energy level that would be unwelcome in many homes.

ALSO SUITED FOR

Family Dog.

CHRISTINE M. PELLICANO

Great Dane

USUAL PLUSES

Debonair, sweet, patient, this breed is breathtaking. We are big fans of Danes. They are wonderful companions that are reliable and stable, but they are also terrific watchdogs. The best among them are not fighters, but dignified, thoughtful dogs that will stand their ground if forced to. With the bellow of their bark and their stunning size, only an idiot would question their authority.

Normally Danes are sweethearts that would rather lean against you for a pat, or shove you off the couch lovingly, than do harm to anyone. They are endlessly focused on, and devoted to, their people.

POSSIBLE DRAWBACKS

Sadly, in many ways this breed is a real mess. Their giant size puts a strain on their health and few males live past 7 or 8. Many die much younger.

In addition, they may suffer some temperament problems, specifically fearfulness. We met one bitch that urinated submissively. Annoying in a Cocker Spaniel, this behavior is a real rug ruiner in a Great Dane! A fearful Dane is a danger to himself and others.

HEIGHT

Females at least 28 inches, males at least 30. Most Danes much larger.

WEIGHT

Ranges according to height, but between 110 and 150 is average.

COLOR

Fawn, brindle, black, blue, harlequin, and Boston marked (black and white, like a Boston Terrier). Merles are also produced in harlequin litters and, as long as their hearing is A-OK, they make fine pets.

GROOMING

Minimal, although daily handling is always a good idea. Get an industrial-sized nail clipper, then have your breeder, vet, or groomer show you how to clip toenails.

SHEDDING

Moderate.

TRAINING

Professional assistance is mandatory because of the size and physical power of this breed. Most are mentally sensitive, making training easy. Because of their size, they respond more slowly to commands than smaller dogs.

Enroll in puppy kindergarten and keep going to training classes until the dog is at least two years old. A confident worldview and immediate response to your verbal command are mandatory for a dog of this size.

EXERCISE

Be careful with hard romps with other dogs or forced exercise, like long walks on-lead, when these dogs are pups. Their fast growth makes them injury-prone. Discuss an appropriate exercise program with your breeder and your veterinarian. Once mature, a couple of brisk half-hour walks a day will do nicely.

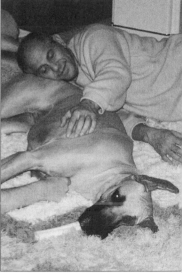

SARAH WILSON

CHILDREN

Usually delightful, especially if raised with older, respectful children. Sheer size-related mishaps are most common. A Cavalier jumps up and scratches a child's legs; a Dane jumps up and knocks the child flat.

OTHER PETS

Good, especially if raised with them. Socialize early and well, for Danes are just too darn big to meet their first cat at ten months.

BITE POTENTIAL

Low to high. Once you've had a good Dane you will never want another breed; once you have had a bad one, you will never want another dog. For some reason, we've met an undue number of very tough, male harlequins.

POSSIBLE HEALTH CONCERNS

Many and serious. Orthopedic problems of every kind, wobblers, von Willebrand's disease, eye problems, thyroid problems, cancer, bloat—the list is positively a parade of diseases. Seek out breeders who check hips, elbows, eyes, and hearts—at a bare minimum.

SPECIAL COMMENTS

Select a smaller Dane. A small Dane is still a *big* dog. Watch that tail! Not only can it clear off tables and whack kids in the face, but that tail tip can also become abraded, a real pain to get healed up.

ALSO SUITED FOR

Watchdog, Nine-to-Five Dog.

Labrador Retriever

USUAL PLUSES

What a fabulous tank of a dog. The classic Lab tolerates children extremely well, is forgiving and sweet. Gun dogs, they can handle loud noise and rough handling better than most—not that they deserve either.

POSSIBLE DRAWBACKS

For a young Labrador life is a contact sport. The very noise and touch tolerance that makes Labs so reliable with kids can make them a challenge to train if you try to use force or intimidation. Yell at a Lab, he'll wag his tail. Swat him, he may wag it even harder. These dogs are terrifically trainable, but you have to work with them, not against them.

Prone to sins of enthusiasm such as jumping up, pulling on-lead, mouthing, stealing objects, and behaving shamelessly around food. All this is manageable with training, exercise, and supervision.

Because of their incredible popularity (number one in the AKC's 1997 ranking with over 150,000 dogs registered), the quality of the dogs ranges widely from wonderful family companion to generally fearful, from hyper triathlete to unpredictably aggressive. Please read the chapter on finding the right dog before you select your companion.

HEIGHT
21½–24½ inches.

WEIGHT
55–80 pounds. (Though this can range wildly. We've met plenty of Labs that tipped the scales with over 100 pounds of lean muscle. Do your research!)

COLOR
Anything from the palest cream through every shade of brown to black. Very occasionally, these dogs have lighter points, similar in look and placement to a Doberman or Rottweiler.

GROOMING
Minimal.

SHEDDING

Moderate.

TRAINING

Absolutely! A truly versatile dog, Labs work as guides for the blind, drug-detection dogs, search-and-rescue animals, and much more. Training gives you control over their sheer exuberance and, more important, a brilliant brain is a terrible thing to waste.

EXERCISE

A lot. For the first three or four years you will be running this dog hard. Fortunately, this isn't difficult. They love to fetch, swim, jog, romp, play at anything—you name it, a good Labrador can do it.

CHILDREN

Good Labradors are wonderfully tolerant. A wide variety of Labs exist, so take the time to find a good one. Supervision and training will help prevent exuberance-related injuries.

OTHER PETS

Should be fine. Occasionally, intact Labs can be tough with other males, so neuter your pets.

BITE POTENTIAL

Low—in a good one. Can be high in a poorly bred or neurotic specimen.

POSSIBLE HEALTH CONCERNS

Hip dysplasia, progressive retinal atrophy, cataracts, and bloat are the things to look out for.

SPECIAL COMMENTS

Be careful of Labradors from strictly field-bred lines. These wiry dogs practically levitate, they have so much energy. While you want this drive and intensity in a field dog, you don't want to live with it in a companion. Dual dogs—with show and field titles behind them—are usually fine for family life.

JENNIFER BRYANT CLAUDIO

ALSO SUITED FOR

High-Input, High-Output Dog; Watchdog; Family Dog.

Toy and Miniature Poodles

USUAL PLUSES

Nonshedding, tiny Einsteins, with all the opinions and behaviors of a larger dog, shrunk into one dynamo of a package. Teach them anything, but don't try to tell these little wizards what they can't do! These dogs are endearing, devoted, happy rays of sunshine.

POSSIBLE DRAWBACKS

Like mindless windup toys, the worst of these breeds just keep going and going without direction, purpose, or ability to stop. "Yappy" does not begin to describe an especially noisy member of these breeds. Generally all of them are barky, but the bad ones take that to a new level of annoying. Aggression is not uncommon.

Miniatures may be a bit calmer than Toys, but we're splitting hairs here. A decent rule of thumb is the more extreme the size, the more problems arise. This applies to both giants and tiny toys.

HEIGHT

10 inches or less for a Toy;
10–15 inches is a Miniature.

WEIGHT

5–7 pounds for Toys,
14–17 pounds for a Miniature.

RENEE EWING

COLOR

Any solid color, though black and white are the most common.

GROOMING

Professional grooming required. Plan to go every couple of months. Fancy haircuts are strictly fashion and not necessary. Feel free to give your Poodle an even shave all over. They are adorable in these "puppy cuts" and very easy to maintain.

SHEDDING

None.

TRAINING

Professional assistance recommended. It is not mandatory because of their small size, but housebreaking, leg lifting, and aggression problems are too common not to get some experienced help. Please do us trainers a favor and get help the very first time you realize a problem is developing. Waiting only makes matters worse.

EXERCISE

Absolutely, although indoor play can suffice. Careful with small puppies leaping off of furniture—legs have been broken that way.

CHILDREN

Toys are too small and too temperamental to be a good bet. Miniatures can be fine with older children.

OTHER PETS

Okay, if raised together. We never recommend large dogs with tiny toys. Although they may get along fine, accidental injury is too easy. Together with another small breed is fine.

BITE POTENTIAL

Moderate to high.

POSSIBLE HEALTH CONCERNS

Pancreatitis, skin problems, allergies, ear infections, eye disorders, subluxating patellas to name a few. These breeds have been popular forever and thus are packed with mediocre animals bred by uninformed people. A good Poodle of any size is an empathetic, charming companion and well worth the happy hunt to find it.

SPECIAL COMMENTS

Don't buy the Teacup Poodles. Don't be suckered in by their cute faces. Behind that adorable look is all too often a compromised mind housed in a compromised body. Buy a normal-sized Toy or larger.

ALSO SUITED FOR

Indoor Companion, Watchdog, Low-Shed Breeds.

How the Poodle Got His Do

The origin of the Poodle haircut is surprisingly utilitarian. When Poodles used to do the work of other retrievers, leaping into water to bring home the owner's prize, their long locks got heavy when wet. To cope with this, owners hacked off the excess. Being sensible people, they left the hair over the joints of the legs and the chest for warmth—the rest went on the floor. Over the years, this proletarian necessity became a patrician affectation, until the Poodle we have left is a powdered and puffed shadow of its former self.

Proceed with caution with these other popular breeds:

Basset Hound

Boxer

Chihuahua

Collie

Dachshund—all

Maltese

Miniature Schnauzer

Pomeranian

Shetland Sheepdog

Shih Tzu

Standard Poodle

Yorkshire Terrier

The Nine-to-Five Dog

Living in an empty home long hours every day is a reality for many dogs. It is not a happy reality for any of them. Some adapt to this life better than others, but no dog enjoys it. If you elect to have a dog under these circumstances, your obligation to that dog increases: You cannot go out for dinner or a movie after work, abandon them on the weekends, or neglect necessary morning and evening exercise routines. Dogs can adjust only so far, then the isolation starts working on them.

The reason dogs make such fabulous companions is that they are social animals. Their need to be with humans is strong. Unless you are willing to select a breed that suits your lifestyle, plan your life around your animal's needs, and be responsible on a daily basis for putting your dog in this unnatural situation—then, please, wait to get your companion. Dogs will always be there. Getting one simply because you "want" one without regard for the dog's needs is cruel—

ROSE MARCHETTI

cruel in the name of "love," but cruel nonetheless. There are other pets that fare better with long hours alone—a pair of cats, for example.

If you have made the decision to add a dog to your life and are willing to take responsibility for all that entails, then here are some breeds that can usually adapt to long periods of isolation with a minimum of stress.

If the nine-to-five dog is underexercised, undertrained, and/or understimulated, you will likely see destructive chewing, nuisance barking or howling, attention-getting behavior, separation anxiety, hyperactivity, fearfulness, and self-mutilation.

Borzoi

USUAL PLUSES

A calm, easygoing, laid-back dog. Strikingly lovely, if you like that art-deco-come-to-life look. Defines elegance and grace. Extremely sweet and loving, on their own terms. Fond of their family, but not normally demanding of a great deal of attention. Usually calm and quiet in the house. Borzoi are not prone to barking incessantly.

POSSIBLE DRAWBACKS

Tall! When these dogs walk up to your dinner table, they look down into your casserole dish. Nothing is safe on a counter. While they are usually sweet, this breed, like some other sighthounds, may not tolerate sudden surprises or pain. Early handling exercises will get your Borzoi used to anything a human might have to do. Borzois are often not watchdogs.

HEIGHT

More than 26 inches
at the shoulder;
often much more.

WEIGHT

55 pounds and up—
and up and up!

COLOR

Any. Usually white plus another color.

GROOMING

Moderate. This is a silky coat. A weekly brushing will keep it trouble free.

SHEDDING

Moderate.

TRAINING

Mandatory. Too big a dog to go untutored. Use positive methods, as sighthounds rarely respond well to anything else. Early handling and socialization will bring out the best in this beautiful animal. Puppy kindergarten is a grand idea. Work on "Come," but don't count on it.

EXERCISE

Moderate. Surprising with such a big dog, but most do very well with a free romp in a fenced area every other day. If well socialized, playing with other dogs is great. If you are a jogger, a Borzoi makes an ideal running partner.

CHILDREN

Maybe. An older, kind dog with a sensible, older kid. Supervise and prevent taunting, as most Borzoi will not tolerate it.

OTHER PETS

Single, well-socialized Borzoi are usually fine with other dogs, though the males can be fighters. Two or more Borzoi can gang up on another animal. Either sex may chase smaller animals.

BITE POTENTIAL

Low to moderate.

POSSIBLE HEALTH CONCERNS

Bloat is the biggest concern. Can be sensitive to medications and flea-control products, so discuss this with your breeder and your veterinarian. Never medicate without express instructions to do so.

SPECIAL COMMENTS

Needs a soft bed or can develop hygromas (large fluid-filled sacs) on pressure points. These hygromas normally go away, but they are quite disconcerting and are best avoided.

ALSO SUITED FOR

City Dog.

English Cocker Spaniel

USUAL PLUSES

Sweet, happy, playful, eager to please—in total, a delightful family companion. Pretty, too, with enough coat to wave merrily when he moves, but not so much that grooming becomes a lifetime project. His tail never stops wagging as he greets everyone like a long-lost pal.

POSSIBLE DRAWBACKS

Some are shy. A few are aggressive. Some have more coat than the breed used to. With these fuzzy ones, set up a regular appointment at your groomer and keep it every two months. With weekly maintenance in between, its coat should be fine.

HEIGHT
15–17 inches.

WEIGHT
26–34 pounds.

COLOR

Almost anything: roan (white with speckles), black and tan, particolor, solid colors. All colors are cute. Don't get hung up on a certain pattern; get the best puppy for you. You'll soon come to love her particular look.

GROOMING

Professional assistance recommended. Ask your groomer about a bikini cut—that is where the dog's belly is cut short but a fringe of hair is left along the edges to give the look, but not the maintenance, of a longer coat. Weekly brushing is mandatory—pay special attention to the belly, back of the hind legs, between the front legs, and behind the ears.

SHEDDING
Moderate.

TRAINING

Always a good idea. English Cockers are so pleased with themselves when they make you happy that their joy alone is reason to teach them. Use positive methods, please—they are too good-natured and sweet for anything else.

EXERCISE

Moderate. Give him a good off-lead romp in a safe, fenced area several times a week plus a few long walks a day and you will be fine.

CHILDREN

Yes, as long as you select a calm, stable pup, then socialize, train, and supervise him properly.

OTHER PETS

Fine with other pets and normally fine with strange dogs.

BITE POTENTIAL

Low.

POSSIBLE HEALTH CONCERNS

Can be prone to ear infections and eye problems. Parents should be CERF, OFA. Some breeders do a BAER test to check for deafness as well. Kidney problems are present in some dogs. The English Cocker Spaniel Club of America is doing commendable work hunting down the genetics of problems.

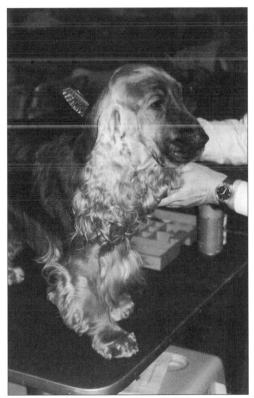

SPECIAL COMMENTS

Can develop cataracts late in life, which lead to blindness.

ALSO SUITED FOR

Family Dog, City Dog.

SARAH WILSON

French Bulldog

USUAL PLUSES

Loving and people-oriented, Frenchies are devoted companions that want to be with you as much as possible. They adapt to country life as well as city life. As long as they have you, they don't care much about their surroundings. This makes them great travelers. Most are not big barkers, though they will certainly let you know when someone is at the door.

POSSIBLE DRAWBACKS

All the snoring, snorting, and farting a short-faced dog can produce. Aggression toward other dogs can be part of your Frenchie, as can predatory tendencies like mousing. Because of the shape of some of these dogs, a few may need their rears wiped after defecation. Because of their build, French Bulldogs sink rather than swim. They are in real danger in the water.

If you choose this breed, be prepared to wait. Breeding is not any easy task. Artificial insemination and C-sections are common, and litters are usually small. This means that Frenchies are not easy to come by. Don't expect them to be inexpensive.

HEIGHT
Around 12 inches.

WEIGHT
19–28 pounds.

COLOR
Brindle (tan with black striping), cream, brindle with white, solid white, fawn.

GROOMING
Minimal. Facial folds may need regular cleaning.

SHEDDING
Moderate.

TRAINING
Recommended. Frenchies have their own opinions. Teaching them to work with you makes them easier to deal with. Teaching self-control helps if they have aggressive tendencies toward other dogs. Don't use slip collars with these dogs, as they can

have tracheal sensitivity. Use either a buckle collar or a small prong, if something stronger is needed.

EXERCISE

Minimal. A couple of brisk fifteen-minute walks a day and a game of fetch in the hallway will keep your Frenchie fit and happy. Keep him indoors during the heat of the day.

CHILDREN

Maybe. Older children with an older dog under supervision. Not all Frenchies are tolerant of a child's handling, so be careful to select a calm, relaxed, easygoing dog.

OTHER PETS

Usually okay if raised with the other animals. Dog aggression may be a problem in some males.

BITE POTENTIAL

Low to moderate.

POSSIBLE HEALTH CONCERNS

Von Willebrand's disease (vWD), thyroid abnormalities, elongated soft palates, and various spine and back problems. If possible, buy your pup from a breeder who X-rays her dogs' spines. Allergies and skin problems are also present.

SPECIAL COMMENTS

Frenchies are heat intolerant, so they're not a good choice for a hot, humid climate. Must be carefully protected from overheating during the summer months. Prone to weight gain. Their protruding eyes can get injured—care is required around children, and cats, and no romps through brush.

ALSO SUITED FOR

City Dog.

JULIA ANNE HAWKINS

Greyhound

USUAL PLUSES

Quiet, dignified, unreasonably sweet—this is a terrific breed for many homes. Greyhounds are rarely aggressive toward people.

There is an extensive network of devoted people who rescue racing Greyhounds from tracks after their career is done. Without this important work, thousands of dogs would be destroyed, and not always humanely. Many seem genuinely grateful for a home and all are crate-trained. Please consider opening your home to one of these dogs if this breed tickles your fancy.

POSSIBLE DRAWBACKS

As with any breed, a range of personalities exists. Select one that matches your family life. They do need long walks and good runs in safe areas several times a week, but they do not demand the kind of exercise you might think. None can be trusted off-lead.

Track Greyhounds often slip into your life with surprising ease. Occasionally one will need help in the housebreaking and chewing departments, but this can be dealt with easily through supervision, a crating schedule, and rewarding the behavior you prefer. Greyhounds are not watchdogs.

HEIGHT
26–30 inches.

WEIGHT
60–70 pounds.

COLOR
Any.

GROOMING
Minimal.

SHEDDING
Minimal.

TRAINING
Why not? Use a positive approach, as they will "shut down" if harsh methods are used. These are sensitive dogs that want to please when not frightened or intimi-

dated. Developing a reasonable recall is mandatory. Start young and keep going! Even with lots of training, the recall may never be good enough to save your dog's life. Keep him fenced in or on a lead.

EXERCISE
Moderate, in a fenced-in area only. These dogs have blistering speed and can be out of your sight in seconds. Often a good run in the morning keeps these dogs content all day.

CHILDREN
Older kids with older dogs. Generally sweet animals, most Greyhounds would rather move away than snap at a child. Greyhounds do not like being manhandled, so if your child is hard to control, or if you tolerate the ridiculous practice of allowing kids to ride on, flop on top of, or generally abuse dogs, then don't get a Greyhound.

OTHER PETS
Usually good with other dogs. Predatory instincts exist in varying degrees, so use caution around cats until you know your particular dog's tendencies. Some may never be able to live safely with smaller animals, but others adapt well.

SARAH WILSON

BITE POTENTIAL
Low.

POSSIBLE HEALTH CONCERNS
Generally healthy dogs. Some hypothyroidism, bloat, hemophilia, bone cancer, and von Willebrand's disease can be found. Their thin, long tails can break, and the tail tips can abrade. Bleeding tail tips are normally caused by wagging against hard objects like doorjambs, and take forever to heal.

SPECIAL COMMENTS
Careful with chemicals. Do not use any flea or tick product unless your veterinarian or Greyhound breeder/rescue person approves it.

ALSO SUITED FOR
Family Dog, City Dog.

Irish Wolfhound

USUAL PLUSES

Such a huge dog nine-to-five? Really? Yes, really, though they are better suited as adults than as pups. Good specimens are calm, sweet dogs that crave your company above that of all others. They are not quarrelsome or difficult, though they are clever and will beg, cajole, and manipulate to get their way.

POSSIBLE DRAWBACKS

This is an extremely sensitive breed. A stern word can send some into quite the depression. Sadly, that sweet sensitivity can become shyness. A seriously shy Wolfhound can be hard to live with. Only accept a calm, confident pup from a calm, confident mother. These dogs are way too big to be hiding under the kitchen table when guests come over. If they become submissive urinators, buy hip boots.

This breed is devastatingly short-lived. A Wolfhound in the double digits is an old hound indeed.

Puppy-proofing your house for a dog that can reach to the top of the refrigerator is a creative chore. Other dogs may react with fear to the IW's size, becoming aggressive even when the IW is completely friendly.

HEIGHT

Males must be at least 32 inches; females, 30 inches.

WEIGHT

Males at least 120 pounds at 18 months; females 105.

COLOR

Gray, brindle, red, fawn. Whites and blacks are rare.

GROOMING

Minimal.

SHEDDING

Minimal.

TRAINING

Absolutely, both because of his sheer size and his sighthound tendency to do what he wants when he wants. Again, use patience and persistence with these gentle hounds.

They are happy to please you if you make yourself clear. Anger or harsh training methods will only confuse and depress them.

EXERCISE

Moderate—a couple of long walks a day and a few off-lead runs a week will do just fine. More is always appreciated.

CHILDREN

Good with good kids, though may knock smaller children over until the IW is taught better manners. IWs are rarely nasty or short-tempered. Most do not enjoy being manhandled and will remove themselves from the situation if they can.

OTHER PETS

Normally fine. Wolfhounds are usually gentle giants.

BITE POTENTIAL

Low.

POSSIBLE HEALTH CONCERNS

Bloat, cancer, hip and elbow problems, epilepsy, tail injury, heart disease.

SPECIAL COMMENTS

That tail can clear off a coffee table in short order.

ALSO SUITED FOR

Family Dog.

VICKI CROKE

Pekingese

USUAL PLUSES

Arrogant, funny, bright, self-possessed, and calm, this is usually a very easy dog to have around. They dote on their chosen people and appreciate the return of that treatment. If you want a dog that thinks he's better than just about anyone—except you, of course—you'll enjoy a Peke. We've been charmed by more than one. These dogs are real characters.

POSSIBLE DRAWBACKS

Some Pekes can be real dominatrices with other dogs. We know one small female that organizes a household of large Labradors with an iron paw. Some aggression is present in the breed, and is most pronounced when they are forced to do anything they do not wish to do. Barking can be a problem.

HEIGHT
8–9 inches.

WEIGHT
About 14 pounds.

COLOR
Any.

GROOMING

Moderate to a lot. The amount of care is directly related to the amount of coat. Males have more fur than females. A thorough weekly brushing should keep things in check. In some dogs, facial folds may need daily attention.

SHEDDING
Moderate.

TRAINING

A lot. This dog needs to know you are a person worth following, or you will quickly be following your Peke. A breed that does not suffer fools gladly, some can be snappish if you do not direct them effectively. Don't use slip collars with these dogs, as they can have tracheal sensitivity. Either use a buckle collar or, if something stronger is needed, a small puppy prong collar.

EXERCISE
Minimal.

CHILDREN
Some may be okay with some children, but not our first choice or, frankly, theirs.

OTHER PETS
Will be tolerated if raised with your Peke. Many Pekes look down on other animals as lesser beings. However, once they find a pal, they are full of comic antics.

ROSE MARCHETTI

BITE POTENTIAL
Moderate. Usually dependable, but if you let them get a high opinion of themselves, they may "correct you" if you step over the line—say, brushing them when they aren't in the mood or bothering them when they are asleep. This is unnecessary behavior and can largely be avoided through socialization and training.

POSSIBLE HEALTH CONCERNS
Prone to some eye problems. Their bulging eyes are prone to injury, which includes, in rare instances, the eyes popping out a bit. Their facial shape leads to breathing problems, some jaw problems. Urinary stones can also crop up

SPECIAL COMMENTS
Watch their weight and protect them from the heat. Overheating can kill a Peke in short order. Experienced people give their Pekes frozen, nontoxic ice packs to lie on.

ALSO SUITED FOR
City Dog, Indoor Companion.

Pug

USUAL PLUSES

Charming, adorable, rarely snippy, we promise you a Pug will make you laugh. As you can tell, we think highly of this dog, though some people fail to look past the exterior to find the canine treasure that lies beneath.

A Pug is a sturdy little dog. He is friendly with most everyone, easygoing, and an all-around pleasant companion.

POSSIBLE DRAWBACKS

Like all short-faced dogs, Pugs may snore, pass gas, and have sensitivity to heat. Some are said to be stubborn, though we haven't had this experience ourselves. Rather, we find that if spoiled, they see no real reason to listen to their owner. This is an owner-caused problem, not a dog-caused one. As pups, these little dogs can be wood-chewing wizards. Crate them and watch them, or your moldings may well suffer.

HEIGHT
10–11 inches.

WEIGHT
Should be 14–18 pounds.

COLOR
Tan with black points, or solid black.

GROOMING
Minimal, though wiping out their facial folds may be necessary.

SHEDDING
A lot—yes, a lot.

TRAINING
Okay, why not? They don't usually need much but they are so comical and smart, why deprive them of the fun? Don't use slip collars with these dogs, as they can have tracheal sensitivity. Use a harness, a buckle collar, or, if something stronger is needed, a puppy prong collar.

EXERCISE

Minimal, but watch their weight!

CHILDREN

Sturdy, loving dog that will normally adore your children. Supervision is a must so that a young child does not injure the dog. Children must be taught that gentle handling is expected. But, in general, if you have problems between the two, they won't be coming from the Pug.

OTHER PETS

Good choice, but don't match them with much larger dogs. Injury is too easy.

BITE POTENTIAL

Low.

POSSIBLE HEALTH CONCERNS

Subluxating patellas, tracheal collapse, epilepsy, hypoglycemia, and, rarely, eyes prolapsing (fancy word for popping out a little). Their facial shape leads to breathing problems and heat intolerance. Heart problems, made worse with obesity, are also present.

SPECIAL COMMENTS

Very sensitive to heat. Keep them cool in the summer. Those facial wrinkles need daily cleaning to avoid infections caused by food getting into them. Watch around young children and cats that their protruding eyes aren't scratched.

SUZANNE KINDER

ALSO SUITED FOR

City Dog, Indoor Companion, Family Dog, Good Dogs That Are Hard to Find.

Shih Tzu

USUAL PLUSES

Through the years, many, many of these dogs have swept us off our feet. Charming, fun-loving, and engaging, these guys will melt your heart.

Shih Tzus are normally gregarious; they like just about everybody and everything. Great fun as travel companions, they will win you friends wherever you go. In our experience, aggression is rare in a well-bred, well-raised Shih Tzu.

POSSIBLE DRAWBACKS

As with many small dogs, housebreaking can be a problem—mostly yours. If your puppy isn't 90 percent clean by four months of age (this is with your careful supervision), get help. Don't wait to see what happens. Let us spare you the suspense: Your rugs will be ruined, your patience will be frayed, your puppy will be confused, and the bond will be stressed.

Brattiness, in the form of disobedience and willful behavior, can develop if they are spoiled, just like it does in humans. Treat them like the smart dogs they are and they will give you years of devoted companionship.

HEIGHT
8–11 inches.

WEIGHT
9–16 pounds.

COLOR
Any.

GROOMING
Professional. We recommend, for your sanity and the dog's comfort, that you keep your dog in a "puppy cut." This is a short body cut with longer hair left on the legs, ears, and tail—quite fetching. Such a cut needs professional attention every few months.

SHEDDING
Minimal.

TRAINING
Okay. Not usually needed for problem control, but this bright breed deserves to be

taught many things. He's such a charmer; why not look into doing pet-therapy work with yours?

EXERCISE

Minimal. Indoor romps are usually plenty. Outdoor exercise is normally enjoyed, but not always required.

CHILDREN

Nice-tempered little dogs that usually like children, if they have been socialized with children. Because of their size and facial shape, Shih Tzus are not suited for toddlers or rough older children.

OTHER PETS

Fine with the Shih Tzu. Careful with larger dogs, though, as injury from play is a real possibility.

BITE POTENTIAL

Low.

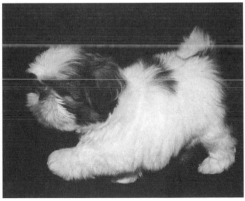

PAULETTE COOPER

POSSIBLE HEALTH CONCERNS

Kidney problems, von Willebrand's disease, and allergies.

SPECIAL COMMENTS

Short-faced, so can get overheated quickly. Careful.

ALSO SUITED FOR

Indoor Companion, City Dog, Good Dogs That Are Hard to Find.

Whippet

USUAL PLUSES

So pretty, so sweet, these elegant running machines were made for speed. Delightful, gentle companion animals, Whippets are clean, quiet, and easy to have around. They are very attached to their people, and generally friendly to others as well. Whippets love nothing better than to have a good run, then curl up next to or on their person for a nap. Expect them to sleep on the bed—they usually want to be under the covers.

POSSIBLE DRAWBACKS

Pups can chew prodigiously if not supervised and crated. Like most sighthounds, they sleep on the furniture, so throw a sheet over the chair and accept the inevitable.

Because they are sensitive, some Whippets can be quite shy. Early socialization, encouraging bravery and ignoring fear, can help your Whippet overcome any natural reticence. Do not—we repeat, do not—coddle! That only reinforces fearful behavior. Also, avoid giving excessive attention during vacations or you can end up with separation anxiety when you go back to work. Whippets are not watchdogs.

HEIGHT
18–22 inches.

WEIGHT
20–35 pounds.

COLOR
Any.

GROOMING
Minimal.

SHEDDING
Minimal.

TRAINING

Okay—they enjoy it *if* it is fun for them. This is a sensitive breed, so use positive methods and you will have fun together. Do not frighten or hurt them in the name of training. Sighthounds are not stupid; they just do not cope with harsh methods as readily as some other breeds.

EXERCISE

Moderate. They all need a good run in a safely fenced area at least every other day; pups need them daily. Long walks on-lead are always good.

CHILDREN

Older children okay, but not a good choice for toddlers who are too rough. Whippets are rarely snappish.

OTHER PETS

Normally fine indoors. Outdoors, these guys are chasers, so watch your cats. Many learn to ignore the feline family members, but some never quite take that rule to heart.

BITE POTENTIAL

Low.

POSSIBLE HEALTH CONCERNS

Hardy breed with few health problems. Careful breeders do X-ray hips and check eyes to make sure their dogs are clear. Can be sensitive to medications and chemicals.

SPECIAL COMMENTS

Will need outerwear in the winter. Whippets do well in pairs.

ALSO SUITED FOR

City Dog, Family Dog.

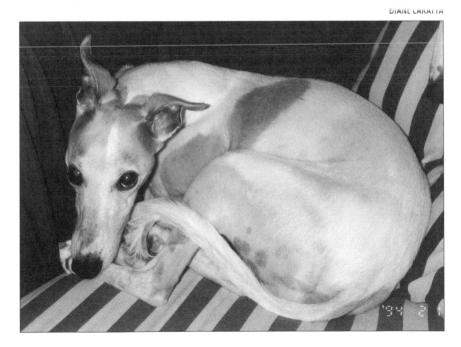

DIANE LARATTA

Other dogs to consider for a nine-to-five lifestyle are:

Bernese Mountain Dog

Bichon Frise

Bullmastiff

Cavalier King Charles Spaniel

Chinese Crested

Great Dane

Great Pyrenees

Japanese Chin

The Family Dog

DIANNE HOPPER

T he family-dog group was the most difficult group to gather. Many of you will be pinning the safety of your children on our recommendations. That is a heavy burden. With that in mind, please read the following carefully.

The breeds selected here may do well in your family, but they may not. First of all, your lifestyle must be taken into account. If no one is home all day and your idea of an athletic outing is to mow the lawn, then a Standard Poodle will likely make you crazy. Second, there are good and bad individuals in every breed. If you find an exceptionally sweet, calm Dalmatian, by all means, get it. We do not think such Dalmatians are as easy to find as Bernese Mountain Dogs. Basically, we play the odds. In our experience, more Berners are likely to be calm, reliable family pets than Dals. Is that a guarantee? No way! Too many factors come into play: your effort, the individual dog, the breeder's priorities, the environment in which you raise the dog, how much training time you invest, the present popularity of the breed, etc.

We selected dogs that are normally tolerant of children, with the lowest overall aggression levels. While considering your options, please also refer to the end of this chapter for other recommendations. The dogs listed there are equally good bets as family companions.

Common problems found in family dogs are food or object stealing, jumping up, assertive licking, mouthing, rough play. All of these unwanted behaviors are usually easily controllable with the proper management and training.

Bernese Mountain Dog

USUAL PLUSES

A more handsome or lovable dog you will be hard-pressed to find. Smart, devoted, easygoing, and adaptable, these dogs just want to be with you. Straightforward to train, these big, tricolor goofballs can steal your heart with one tongue-lolling grin. An added but largely irrelevant detail is that the puppies look like stuffed toys: excessively cute.

POSSIBLE DRAWBACKS

Sadly, this wonderful breed has its fair share of hip dysplasia and weak temperaments. These temperaments can take the form of either extreme shyness or assertive behavior. Since this is a large breed, assertiveness, which can lead to aggression, is completely unacceptable. Select a calm, stable pup from calm, stable parents.

HEIGHT
23–27½ inches.

WEIGHT
Around 65–90 pounds, some larger.

COLOR
Always mostly black with tan and white markings.

GROOMING
Moderate; a weekly brushing does the trick most of the time. During shedding season, expect to invest more time and effort and brush a few times a week.

SHEDDING
Moderate except twice a year, when it is profuse.

TRAINING
Strongly suggested. This dog wants to please and deserves to know precisely how he can. Remember: The larger the dog, the greater your responsibility.

EXERCISE
Moderate. A couple of long, brisk walks a day and a good romp in a safe area are plenty. Younger dogs need more exercise, but it shouldn't be forced. Ask your breeder or veterinarian what would be an appropriate program.

CHILDREN
A good Berner is excellent with well-mannered, well-supervised children.

OTHER PETS
Usually fine.

BITE POTENTIAL
Low to high—more are low than high.

POSSIBLE HEALTH CONCERNS
Hip and elbow dysplasia, cancer, bloat, and orthopedic problems. Sadly, this is another short-lived breed; a decade is about the most you can expect.

SPECIAL COMMENTS
Numbers are on the rise. Berners may well be one of the next "hot" breeds. Ringing in at 71st out of 137 in 1993, they are at 62nd in 1997. This is bad news for Bernese lovers everywhere. Proceed with caution when researching and acquiring this dog.

ALSO SUITED FOR
Watchdog, Nine-to-Five Dog.

ROSEMARY GLADSTAR

Cavalier King Charles Spaniel

USUAL PLUSES

Cavaliers are wonderful, happy animals with a tail like a metronome. A breed big enough to keep up with anything you want to do but small enough for a child to walk (under supervision). Aggression problems are extremely rare, though popularity may change that.

These dogs live to please you. They are a wonderful choice as a companion for all ages. They adore being with you, traveling with you, curling up on your lap at the end of the day, or chasing a toy. Few things on this earth are as charming as the grinning face of a happy Cavalier.

POSSIBLE DRAWBACKS

Careful of shy ones. Select confident, happy puppies from confident, happy adults. If the pup's mother is less than outgoing, don't buy one of her pups. A Cavalier is so darn cute you may overindulge it both with attention and with food. Steel yourself not to.

HEIGHT
12–13 inches.

WEIGHT
13–18 pounds.

COLOR

Blenheim (chestnut and white), black and tan (predominantly black with tan over eyes, on cheeks, chest, legs, underside of tail, and underside of ears), ruby (rich red), tricolor (white dog with black patches and tan markings the same as in black and tan).

GROOMING

Little to moderate. Fine hair around ears and britches can tangle if not combed out weekly. This task, if kept up with, should not take more than a few minutes. More heavily coated dogs require more care.

SHEDDING
Moderate.

TRAINING

Little necessary, though all appreciated! These sweet dogs do not require much to civilize them, but they are so eager to please and bright it's a shame to let that intelligence go to waste.

EXERCISE

Little necessary, but willing and able to do just about anything you have in mind. Some brisk walking and indoor play will keep most Cavaliers happy, but I know many that compete in agility, and some that even work as gun dogs retrieving birds almost as big as they are! Don't underestimate them.

CHILDREN

Good with good kids. Bread and butter don't go together better. All children and dogs require supervision and education to treat each other kindly, but in most situations this is a wonderful pairing.

OTHER PETS

Fine. Most will chase small animals when out-of-doors, but few would harm such quarry were they to catch up with it.

BITE POTENTIAL

Low, and with any luck the breed will stay that way.

POSSIBLE HEALTH CONCERNS

Subluxating patellas and serious heart problems are prevalent. Buy only from cardiac-tested parents.

SPECIAL COMMENTS

As much as we hate to say this because we know what popularity can do to a breed, this is a dog that can and does fit into a wide range of lifestyles without a yip.

SARAH WILSON

ALSO SUITED FOR

City Dog, Nine-to-Five Dog.

Collie—Both Rough and Smooth Varieties

USUAL PLUSES

A good Collie is a loving, loyal, trainable dog that gets along with all family members—man or beast. Collies are alert, playful, and want to please. Their sensitivity, both physical and mental, makes them easier to train than some of the less sensitive sporting breeds.

POSSIBLE DRAWBACKS

Lassie did Collies no favors. Rampant and indiscriminate breeding has created some mighty neurotic Collies. These dogs can have a myriad of behavior problems, perhaps the most annoying of which is spinning in a circle while barking. Some Collies snap if startled or threatened. They can be reserved with people outside the family, and some can be fearful.

HEIGHT
24–26 inches.

WEIGHT
50–75 pounds.

COLOR

Most commonly sable (tan) and white, next is black tri (mostly black with white and tan markings). Less common are the merle (gray, black, and white all mixed together) and the white (predominantly white with a few sable, tricolor, or merle markings).

GROOMING

Rough variety: A lot. A thorough weekly brushing can take you half an hour or more, but it must be done.

Smooth variety: Moderate. Both types can be prone to hot spots (acute skin irritations that crop up overnight), especially in hot, humid climates.

SHEDDING

Rough-Coat: A whole lot. Smooth-Coat: Moderate.

TRAINING

Recommended, to build confidence and trust. No harsh methods—this is generally a soft breed; just show him what you want, he'll do it. Socialization is very important. Start with puppy class and continue. You'll both enjoy it and the benefit will be a confident dog who is a joyous companion.

EXERCISE

Mandatory, especially when young. As herding dogs, Collies can be chasers, so exercise them in safe areas.

CHILDREN

Good to not so good, depending on the stability of the dog you select and the socialization you give him.

CARLA CARO

OTHER PETS

Should be fine.

BITE POTENTIAL

Low to high, depending on the dog.

POSSIBLE HEALTH CONCERNS

Collie eye anomaly—it takes a prevalent problem to get named after a breed. In fact, estimates say that some 95 percent of Collies carry or have this problem. Never buy a Collie unless her parents' eyes are tested.

Dermatomyositis is another common Collie problem, with well over half the population being carriers or affected. It is an autoimmune skin disorder that begins with lesions and skin ulcers on the face. It can progress into muscular atrophy that makes chewing or swallowing difficult. Other problems, if you need more, include progressive retinal atrophy and Collie nose, an ulcerated condition on the nose.

SPECIAL COMMENTS

Can be jumpers; may need more than a five-foot fence to contain them. Ask your veterinarian and breeder about how to handle heartworm medications, as some Collies appear to be sensitive to some medications.

ALSO SUITED FOR

Good Dogs That Are Hard to Find, Watchdog.

English Setter

USUAL PLUSES

Lovely, easygoing dog, by far our favorite setter. Enjoys being with your family; isolating these kind souls will break their hearts. Eager to please, they learn commands easily. Mature dogs are normally calm in the house and absolutely gorgeous romping outside. This is the least popular of the three setters, though we can't for the life of us imagine why.

POSSIBLE DRAWBACKS

Field-bred dogs can be too active and high-energy to live with easily. Long hours alone can cause chewing, barking, or hyperactivity problems, especially in young dogs. Crate training is strongly recommended, combined with regular daily exercise. Some may be a bit slow to housebreak, but this is not usually a horrible problem.

HEIGHT
24–25 inches.

WEIGHT
45–70 pounds.

COLOR

White with tan, brown, or black flecks.

GROOMING

A lot. These dogs vary in amount of coat. Some have a great deal and will need a thorough brush-out several times a week. Others have less. That neat, dapper look will only be achieved through regular visits to the groomer for clipping.

SHEDDING
Moderate.

TRAINING

Moderate. Use positive methods, and these dogs will comply. Creating fear or pain is a good way to confuse a setter. These are not stupid dogs; rather, they are gentle dogs who respond best to kind, fair training.

EXERCISE

High. Especially when young, this dog needs a good run twice a day in a fenced area. Even long walks on-lead will not do the trick. Normally a social dog, he plays well with others.

CHILDREN

Good choice. These dogs are rarely aggressive, and in most circumstances sweetness prevails.

OTHER PETS

Should be fine.

BITE POTENTIAL

Low.

POSSIBLE HEALTH CONCERNS

Deafness and progressive retinal atrophy.

SPECIAL COMMENTS

Some of these dogs can be sensitive to vaccines, so discuss this with your breeder and vet.

ALSO SUITED FOR

High-Input, High-Output Dog.

CHRISTINE M. PELLICANO

Keeshond

USUAL PLUSES

Alert, happy, fun-loving, medium-sized dogs, Keeshonden get along well with other animals and people. Most are stable dogs that enjoy life to the fullest.

A Kees wants to be with people all the time—if not you, then the neighbor will do fine. Known for being gentle and nonaggressive, Kees are generally gregarious. When he can't be out participating, he will perch by a window and comment on everything going on outside.

POSSIBLE DRAWBACKS

Can be barky. Loads of hair to deal with during shedding season. Some are hard to housebreak, so keep to the routine and make friends with your crate. If you have a hectic household, find a calmer breed. High-energy households tend to make this high-energy breed even more active.

HEIGHT

17–18 inches.

WEIGHT

35–40 pounds.

COLOR

Gray with black highlights.

GROOMING

A proper Keeshond coat does not mat much, except at shedding or at a puppy's coat change. The rest of the time, a thorough once-a-week brushing should be fine.

SHEDDING

During shedding you will brush a great deal and not make much of a dent in the problem, but that is only twice a year, so it is bearable.

TRAINING

Absolutely. Intelligent and full of whimsy, he will remind you not to take this all too seriously. Have fun and no Kees will be able to resist you.

EXERCISE

Vital. These are vigorous, vivacious dogs that thrive on activity. Keep them in the cool, though; their thick coat does them no favors in the heat.

CHILDREN

Generally good. Has a well-deserved reputation for being excellent with children. Please do not take this as carte blanche to harass them; they are still dogs.

OTHER PETS

Generally good.

BITE POTENTIAL

Low.

POSSIBLE HEALTH CONCERNS

Generally healthy. Occasionally you may see hip dysplasia, thyroid, skin problems, or diabetes. Epilepsy can be a problem, but it has been diminished in the breed.

SARAH WILSON

SPECIAL COMMENTS

Many Kees smile, flashing a toothy grin when happy. With all that coat, they can overheat in the summer, so be careful.

ALSO SUITED FOR

City Dog, Watchdog.

Newfoundland

USUAL PLUSES

Laid-back, good-natured giant whose main dream in life consists of doing something—anything—with you, then napping in a cool spot afterwards. Highly trainable, these are patient, people-oriented dogs that need to be part of your life. No breed deserves to be isolated in a backyard, but such treatment would break a Newf's heart. Things the Newf excels at include backpacking, cart-pulling, obedience-competing, baby-sitting, and owner-loving.

POSSIBLE DRAWBACKS

Jumbo size, some drool (especially males), loads of hair to deal with. If dirt in your home makes you cringe, this is not your breed. Many, even most, are short-lived.

While this is a big, *big* dog, they are not doltish. These are smart, mentally active dogs that need work. Left to their own devices, the amount of damage a bored Newf can do is extraordinary. If you play rough games with your puppy, be ready to pay the price with the adult dog. While it may seem charming to wrestle with a 45-pound pup, when your adult plays that game, you will be gleefully flattened.

This is a true working breed. If you want to really understand the nature of these animals, work with them.

HEIGHT

26–28 inches.

WEIGHT

110–150 pounds; some are much larger.

COLOR

Most common is solid black. Next in line comes Landseer (white with black patches) or bronze. Most rare are the grays.

GROOMING

What do you think?

SHEDDING

Incomprehensible if you aren't brushing regularly. We've walked into Newf-owning homes to see clumps of hair stuck to the wall, cemented in place by Newf slobber.

TRAINING

Mandatory simply because of the bulk, power, and enthusiasm of this breed. Develop and maintain verbal control at a young age. Crate training is a must.

EXERCISE

Mandatory as a young dog, moderate with an adult. Up to two years old or so, your gigantic puppy needs a twice-daily workout to be his best in your home. Swimming is ideal, both because he naturally loves it and because it is gentle on his rapidly growing frame. Ask your veterinarian or breeder about the best exercise routine for your new companion.

CHILDREN

Absolutely, but be aware that a slobbery slurp from a Newf will knock your average toddler down. Even the most enthusiastic dog-loving child may not like that. The dogs themselves usually take their role as canine nanny quite seriously; they are known for being attentive and loving toward children.

OTHER PETS

Absolutely. This is a gentle breed.

BITE POTENTIAL

Low.

POSSIBLE HEALTH CONCERNS

Bloat, heat sensitivity, hip dysplasia, elbow dysplasia, allergies, SAS (subaortic stenosis).

SPECIAL COMMENTS

The Newfoundland Club of America is a forward-thinking organization, spending time, energy, and money researching the genetic problems in this breed. They encourage a well-rounded, hardworking, healthy dog.

ALSO SUITED FOR

High-Input, High-Output Dog (kind of).

MARIAN ADAMS

Samoyed

USUAL PLUSES

Friendly, happy, people-oriented, these stunning white Nordic dogs are accepting, loving members of the family. Generally tolerant, they don't have a bone to pick with either man or beast. Few dogs have the range of facial expressions that sled dogs do—when happy, they positively grin.

POSSIBLE DRAWBACKS

Dogs of Nordic origin dig and bark, a tendency made worse by boredom. Not outside dogs to be ignored and isolated, Sammys need to be with you. Housebreaking can be a bit of a challenge, so start early and keep at it. Once they understand, they are very clean dogs.

HEIGHT
19–23½ inches.

WEIGHT
50–75 pounds.

COLOR
White, cream, biscuit.

GROOMING

Not as difficult as other softer-coated breeds, this functional coat needs a thorough brushing a couple of times a week. During shedding, brush more or mats will win. Despite being white, these coats tend to shed dirt surprisingly well.

SHEDDING

Twice a year, a lot. Rest of the year, moderate with proper brushing and diet.

TRAINING

Good idea. These are sensitive dogs that will tune you out if you come on too strong or too weak. Be a clear, kind, and consistent leader and they will give you your due. Quite bright; it will not be lack of intelligence that holds you back.

EXERCISE

A lot when young. Given a couple of long walks a day and a romp, they are usually fairly calm. Even so, they will dig simply because they enjoy digging.

CHILDREN
Usually a nice match.

OTHER PETS
Should be fine.

BITE POTENTIAL
Low.

POSSIBLE HEALTH CONCERNS
Hip and eye problems do exist, so purchase pups from breeders who do testing.

SPECIAL COMMENTS
Barking can be controlled through selection, exercise, training, and company. Controlled, but not eliminated. Breed club is active in the education of its members regarding genetic disease. Good for them!

ALSO SUITED FOR
Watchdog.

CHRISTINE M. PELLICANO

Standard Poodle

USUAL PLUSES

Another dog for all seasons. We both adore this elegant, talented breed and implore you not to allow the haircuts inflicted on them by the fashion-crazed show world to affect your opinion of this fine, fine dog. They are at the top of the smart scale, willing to please, athletic, great watchdogs with an endless interest in everything.

POSSIBLE DRAWBACKS

Can be overly protective of their owners. Some people think "Oh, a Poodle being protective, how charming." It isn't! This is a large, smart, athletic breed, and you will have your hands full if you allow this behavior to develop. Their biggest drawback is their hair-based reputation as sissy dogs. Not so. They were originally working retrievers that still like to work and swim. They are also burdened by a myriad of health problems that come with their years of popularity.

HEIGHT

More than 15 inches
at the shoulder.

WEIGHT

Usually 45–75 pounds.

COLOR

Solid colors only. From white to black and everything in between.

GROOMING

Extensive. Professional grooming is mandatory. Should see a groomer every 6 to 8 weeks. Will need brushing and baths in between.

SHEDDING

None.

TRAINING

Mandatory. Not because they are difficult, but because they are so darn smart. Either you give them things to do or they will set about training you—a task they do well.

EXERCISE

A lot, especially those first few years.

CHILDREN

Usually a good choice, though the dog will have to learn to control its natural exuberance. There is a wide range of temperaments out there, so select carefully.

OTHER PETS

Usually fine, if raised with the other pet. Some Poodles, of both sexes, can be tough with other dogs.

BITE POTENTIAL

Low to high. Popularity has created a lot of Poodles, not all of them wonderful. Good ones are wonderful; poorly bred dogs are neurotic disappointments.

DAVID EGEN

COMMON HEALTH PROBLEMS

Hip dysplasia, eye problems, bloat, epilepsy, sebaceous andenitis, Addison's disease, and thyroid problems. Your fantasy pup comes from long-lived, bloat-free parents that have X-rayed hips and are CERF clear, von Willebrand's disease normal, thyroid normal, and have had skin-punch biopsies. Don't count on finding such a dog—but it is nice to dream.

SPECIAL COMMENTS

Royal Standards are an invention of the marketplace and are not recognized by the AKC. Bigger is not better. Shop for health and temperament, and we promise you that you will fall in love with this breed whether it is 24 or 28 inches tall. The Poodle Club of America is to be commended for its commitment to understanding and tracking genetic disease in their breed(s).

ALSO SUITED FOR

Low-Shed Breed, Watchdog, Good Dogs That Are Hard to Find.

Welsh Springer Spaniel

USUAL PLUSES

A delightful, lesser-known spaniel. Medium-sized, multipurpose companion for anything you're game for. Welshies do well in obedience, agility, and hunting trials, they make good jogging companions, and much more. Sweet, tail-wagging animals, these dogs are a bit more owner-attached than the typical American Cocker or the English Springer Spaniel.

POSSIBLE DRAWBACKS

Early socialization and training will bring out the best in your Welshie. They can be a bit shy and sensitive, so you need early work to counteract that tendency. This is one of the rarest breeds we list, so you may have to hunt for a breeder, then be prepared to wait for a puppy.

HEIGHT
16–17 inches.

WEIGHT
38–45 pounds.

COLOR
Always white and red.

GROOMING
Moderate.

SHEDDING
Moderate.

TRAINING
Moderate—needs consistent socialization. Since a Welshie is eager and willing to please you, training is great fun. Adaptable to many methods; positive ones bring out the best.

EXERCISE
Moderate to a lot. This is an active but not hyperactive breed. Daily romps and decent walks will normally keep this breed quite happy.

CHILDREN

Good choice—if dogs are selected, socialized, and supervised properly.

OTHER PETS

Usually fine.

BITE POTENTIAL

Low.

POSSIBLE HEALTH CONCERNS

Epilepsy, glaucoma, progressive retinal atrophy, and ear infections.

SPECIAL COMMENTS

Recently seen in several TV commercials—we fear that their popularity will increase. If it does, proceed with the normal popularity-related caution when researching a puppy.

ALSO SUITED FOR

High-Input, High-Output Dog

MICHAEL STEIGERWALD

Here are other breeds we like equally well for families who are willing to do the research, training, socialization, and management necessary to develop a really fine family companion. You will not find many under fifteen pounds in this group. This is more for the dog's protection than for the child's. The * denotes dogs that do best with older children.

Bearded Collie*

Bichon Frise*

Brittany

Bullmastiff*

English Cocker Spaniel

Flat-Coated Retriever

Golden Retriever

Greyhound

Irish Wolfhound

Labrador Retriever

Norfolk Terrier*

Norwich Terrier*

Pembroke Welsh Corgi*

Portuguese Water Dog

Pug*

Shetland Sheepdog*

Whippet*

"Help! I Failed Dog School"

Not every dog/owner team is cut out to be in a training class. That doesn't mean your dog is stupid or bad. He may be easily distracted, fearful, or aggressive toward others. *You* may not learn well through verbal instruction. Or—horror of horrors—the trainer may not teach very well. Trainers who can't teach often have students who don't learn.

If you did not get what you'd hoped for from training class, why not try a few private lessons? Once both of you have some knowledge under your belt, then you can try another class.

The High-Input, High-Output Dog

The high-input, high-output dogs are the get-up-and-go dogs, the run-five-miles-then-play-a-game-of-Frisbee dogs, the triathletes and the marathoners. Do not get one of these unless you already have an active lifestyle.

These dogs want to be with you as much as possible. If you want a dog to lie at your feet, amuse itself, and be happy alone nine-to-five after a short morning walk, look elsewhere. If you want a dog that lives life to the fullest and wants you to, too, these are the canines for you!

Many of these dogs are extremely intelligent. Owning one is a use-it-or-lose-it situation. Either you harness that intelligent mind through training, or he will use it to develop behaviors you would rather not see. Common problems associated with these dogs are largely management issues that can be attributed to inadequate exercise, improper socialization, or poor training/management habits: chewing, wandering, nuisance barking, hyperactivity, attention-getting behaviors, digging, jumping up, mouthing.

LEWIS HIZER

Alaskan Malamute

USUAL PLUSES

Big, good-natured goofs, most of the time. Funny dogs with a great sense of humor, they can cajole you out of being serious with them. The most powerful of the Nordic breeds, they are great backpacking companions and weight-pulling competitors. But if you want a dog that responds instantly to your commands, never gets into trouble, and thinks only of you, try another breed.

POSSIBLE DRAWBACKS

These are powerful dogs with their own minds. They can be mentally resistant to training unless you are 100 percent consistent and fair, and you make sense to the dog. Don't expect them to practice meaningless exercises endlessly. The best approach is to integrate training into daily life and link the dog's response with getting what he wants. If a Mal understands what to do and why to do it, he will comply.

Malamutes can be aggressive in many ways: predatory, possessive, dog-to-dog. They are not usually aggressive with people unless you pick a fight with them. Prone to chewing, digging, and disturbing the peace when bored.

HEIGHT
23–25 inches.
Some can be much bigger.

WEIGHT
75–110 muscular pounds.

COLOR
Black, gray, silver, red, or, rarely, white.

GROOMING
Thorough brushing once a week or so should be fine.

SHEDDING
During shedding (the exact timing of which is an individual matter), forget pristine housekeeping because there will be hair everywhere. Expect to vacuum the house daily. A good twice-a-day brushing will keep the worst at bay, but it will not eliminate the fuzz bunnies that will be rolling under your couch and gathering in the corners. The good news is that it's only a couple of weeks, twice a year.

TRAINING

Professional assistance is mandatory. This is a powerful dog with a mind of his own. Convince him early that you are worth following, then never let him think otherwise. Do not resort to violence. If you do, you may win the battle but you will lose the war.

EXERCISE

Mandatory, daily, and vigorous.

SARAH WILSON

CHILDREN

A good specimen of the breed that is well socialized and supervised is usually okay with good kids. Because of the sheer knockdown potential, not recommended for small children.

OTHER PETS

Can fight with other dogs; never put together two intact animals of the same sex. If raised with other animals, usually fine indoors. Outdoors, most will give chase if they see something small moving fast.

BITE POTENTIAL

Moderate.

POSSIBLE HEALTH CONCERNS

Hip dysplasia, bloat, dwarfism, and hypothyroidism.

SPECIAL COMMENTS

We happen to enjoy this breed. We have also seen some spectacular mental battles between Mals and their owners, usually caused by the owner attempting to "show the dog who's boss." FYI: In all cases, the owners lost.

ALSO SUITED FOR

Not for Everyone.

Bearded Collie

USUAL PLUSES

Bouncing Beardies! Their slogan? "Gravity is a bummer." Gleeful, enthusiastic, clownish; if a Beardie fails to make you smile, you are really in a foul mood. Bright, trainable, always ready to boldly go where no dog's gone before!

This dog will love you with abandon, and will feel warm toward your neighbors as well. Their job description calls for "tireless," and they are darn close to that. For all their energy, they are normally gentle souls that enjoy nothing more than spending time with you.

POSSIBLE DRAWBACKS

Muddy pawprints everywhere! When long-locked Beardies are wet, they bring a lot of water into your home. Keep a towel or two by the door. Your house and your car will never be quite the same. Barking was part of their job description years back, so expect it now.

Beardies can be sound-sensitive and shy, so socialize them carefully. Seek professional guidance if your dog shows a strong startle response to sound and does not recover quickly.

HEIGHT
20–22 inches.

WEIGHT
About 45–55 pounds.

COLOR
Black, gray, brown, and fawn. Color lightens with age.

GROOMING
The correct harsh coat needs brushing a couple of times a week to stay tangle-free. A softer coat needs more frequent brushing to prevent mats. When changing from puppy to an adult coat, near daily brushing is required. Clipping the hair short will make both your lives easier.

SHEDDING
Moderate.

TRAINING

Mandatory. Youth is a joyous time for a Beardie, and it can be a trying one for an owner. The ability to direct your pup's actions is key to your sanity and his. Trainable in the extreme, shared communication will bring great pleasure to both of you. If you are rough with them, they may well resist the work.

EXERCISE

Mandatory. Remember that "tireless" trait we mentioned above? Young dogs need at least two long romps a day off-lead in a safe area. Playing with other dogs is ideal. Long walks, along with training, are not extras but necessities for these vigorous dogs.

SARAH WILSON

CHILDREN

Usually fine, though sins of glee are common. Because of this, we think infants and toddlers are out; larger, sturdier, better-coordinated children are in.

OTHER PETS

Usually fine.

BITE POTENTIAL

Low to moderate.

POSSIBLE HEALTH CONCERNS

Generally healthy. Some hip dysplasia, progressive retinal atrophy, Addison's disease, hypothyroidism, von Willebrand's disease. None is prevalent.

SPECIAL COMMENTS

The only problems we see with this breed are sound-sensitivity on the dog's part and energy underestimation on the owner's part.

ALSO SUITED FOR

Family Dog, Watchdog.

Belgian Sheepdog

USUAL PLUSES

Highly trainable, very devoted, and scary-smart dogs. We also happen to think they are handsome. We've seen many much adored by single people or childless couples who have the time to devote to the training, exercise, and supervision this special breed requires.

POSSIBLE DRAWBACKS

All the Belgian breeds—Tervuren, Sheepdog, and Malinois—are mentally and physically quick. Many tend to trot in circles while on-lead. Why? It's a herding breed! Circling, keeping everyone together, worrying about wanderers are all part of the territory.

This is a breed that needs daily work and calm—we repeat, calm—management. If you are an emotional, nervous person, you will make this dog nuts.

Can be overprotective, generally aggressive, hyperactive, nervous, shy, flighty, and highly distractible. If poorly trained and underexercised, expect destructive chewing, barking, heel nipping, jumping, and other obnoxious results. Very territorial; will race and bark on the fence line if allowed.

HEIGHT
22–26 inches.

WEIGHT
Around 60–75 pounds.

COLOR
Black.

GROOMING
A lot.

SHEDDING
Moderate, except when shedding season is upon you—then a lot.

TRAINING
Professional assistance is mandatory. Start young and continue for his lifetime. Daily work and consistent management are sine qua non with this breed.

EXERCISE

Mandatory. Over an hour a day, every day. More on the weekends. And we don't mean sedate walks on-lead, either. A fenced-in area for exercise is a must.

CHILDREN

Okay with older children if raised with them, trained properly (both the kids and the dog), and supervised intelligently. May not tolerate mauling by toddlers with good humor.

OTHER PETS

Can be fine if raised with them and trained properly. Bored, unstable, or predatory Belgians may be unreliable with smaller animals.

BITE POTENTIAL

Moderate to high.

POSSIBLE HEALTH CONCERNS

Generally healthy—some hip dysplasia and epilepsy. Hot spots (moist, raw skin lesions) and flea allergies can be a challenge.

SPECIAL COMMENTS

The Belgian Sheepdog Club really encourages versatility in the breed. That kind of support for both beauty and brains is wonderful.

ALSO SUITED FOR

Not for Everyone, Watchdog.

SARAH WILSON

Boxer

USUAL PLUSES

A Boxer's T-shirt would read AIRBORNE AND LOVING IT. Playful, physical, generally good-natured, willing to please, these athletic dogs are good fun if you like to play. They are companionable dogs that want to nap next to you while you both snore, jog with you while you both wheeze, and romp with you till both of you are gasping for breath.

POSSIBLE DRAWBACKS

There is a wide range of temperaments, so be sure to select a calmish, confident pup from a sensible mother. A hyperactive or aggressive Boxer is a challenge. Many Boxers have dog-aggressive tendencies, so socialize, train, and take precautions. Boxers are bold and pushy by nature. Aficionados find their exuberance charming; newcomers can find it overwhelming. This breed is on the rise, growing from 17th in 1993 to 13th in 1997. Poor specimens are being produced. Be careful!

HEIGHT
21–25 inches.

WEIGHT
60–75 pounds.

COLOR

Tan to brindle (brown with black stripes). Occasionally a white boxer is born. Watch for deafness with the whites, but otherwise they make fine pets.

GROOMING
Minimal.

SHEDDING
Minimal to moderate.

TRAINING

Mandatory. This high-energy breed needs calm, consistent direction to help him develop much-needed self-control. Yelling or hitting on your part is likely to increase the dog's activity level, not calm him. Early training and socialization is mandatory. Can be mouthy as pups.

EXERCISE

Mandatory. A lot, at least twice a day. Off-leash romps in safe areas, especially with other dogs, help him a great deal.

CHILDREN

Yes, if the child is large enough to deal with an exuberant, life-is-a-contact-sport dog. A young Boxer with a young child is not the easiest match.

OTHER PETS

Okay, if raised with them. Boxers may fight with other dogs; don't put two dogs of the same sex or same age in the same house.

BITE POTENTIAL

Low to moderate.

POSSIBLE HEALTH CONCERNS

Bloat, cancer, gum and dental problems, fatal colitis problems, eye problems (Boxer ulcer), back degeneration, and SAS (subaortic stenosis). Short-lived, often under ten years. Like all short-muzzled dogs, Boxers may snort, snore, and pass gas. They are prone to heat stress; not the jogging companion for hot summer days.

SARAH WILSON

SPECIAL COMMENTS

We see more and more Boxers with uncut ears. We think this is a terrific trend.

ALSO SUITED FOR

Watchdog, Good Dogs That Are Hard to Find.

Brittany

USUAL PLUSES

Medium-sized, athletic, and active, this is usually a lovely dog for an active family. Normally sensitive to verbal tone, this dog is not hard to manage if exercised enough. Does not need, nor does he respond well to, harsh words.

Playful, curious, and busy, this dog is ready for anything at all times. He is generally good with other animals and fine with people. He may or may not be wildly friendly to strangers, but he is not normally aggressive.

POSSIBLE DRAWBACKS

Be on the lookout for shyness problems. Select a happy, stable pup from happy, stable adults. This dog needs exercise, especially the first few years. Britts are not couch potatoes, and they're not for couch potatoes. If left alone long hours every day or underexercised, you will see the worst in this dog. Under those conditions, expect hyperactivity, restlessness, chewing, jumping, and other obnoxious behaviors.

The Brittany can be mentally sensitive, which often makes him easy to train with voice tone. On the downside, the Brittany is not always the right choice for hectic, noisy households. Investing your effort in early and extensive socialization will reap you years of benefits.

HEIGHT
17½–20½ inches.

WEIGHT
30–40 pounds.

COLOR
Orange and white, or liver and white.

GROOMING
Minimal.

SHEDDING
Moderate.

TRAINING

Recommended. Early socialization and an upbeat puppy class will start your Britt off on the right paw. Use positive methods and this breed will give you his heart. If you stay calm, you'll find him a quick study.

EXERCISE

High. Daily runs—plural—are absolutely necessary.

CHILDREN

Good with good kids. Teach your children to be gentle and to respect a dog when he moves away, and you shouldn't have a lot of problems. Chase this dog, frighten this dog, or corner him, and you will leave him with few behavioral options other than aggression. Use puppy tests to select a calm, physically resilient Brittany.

OTHER PETS

Should be fine.

BITE POTENTIAL

Low.

POSSIBLE HEALTH CONCERNS

Hip dysplasia, epilepsy, and glaucoma.

SPECIAL COMMENTS

Not always the best choice for the city because of their exercise needs and their sensitivity. If constantly stressed by city life, Brittanys can become nervous.

ALSO SUITED FOR

Family Dog.

KATHIE BRANDON

Flat-Coated Retriever

USUAL PLUSES

Another great retriever with all the great retriever qualities, like sound and touch tolerance, trainability, and a low aggression level. Happy, exuberant, people-loving, a Flat-Coat has never met a stranger. He is ready for everything from hunting tests to agility (competition where the dog races over an obstacle course), tracking to obedience. This is a truly versatile breed.

POSSIBLE DRAWBACKS

If you want a dog that matures into dignified calmness, look elsewhere. Flat-Coats are happy for years! This is a breed that benefits greatly from mental structure and regular, daily exercise. Allowed to do as he pleases, he will drag you around, harass you to play with him, chew just about everything, dig holes to China, and generally be an active, good-natured pest. Because these dogs are so people-oriented, separation anxiety can be a problem. They don't usually make the best nine-to-five dogs.

Flat-Coats may be hard to find. Expect to wait once you do locate a breeder you like and to pay more than you would for a Labrador or a Golden.

HEIGHT
22–24½ inches.

WEIGHT
About 55–80 pounds.

COLOR
Solid black or solid dark brown (called liver).

GROOMING
Minimal. A weekly brushing will do nicely.

SHEDDING
Moderate.

TRAINING
Mandatory, to direct his energy and enthusiasm. We haven't yet met one with evil in his heart, but we have met plenty that were rude, ill mannered, and overly physical.

EXERCISE

A lot and daily. An hour or so in the morning and evening is about right.

CHILDREN

Generally tolerant of kids, though no dog should have to suffer teasing or torment. Because little children can get exuberance-related injuries with this breed, the Flat-Coat may be better suited to older kids. Toy and clothing stealing needs to be redirected early or it can become a real sport for a Flat-Coat.

OTHER PETS

Should be fine.

BITE POTENTIAL

Low.

POSSIBLE HEALTH CONCERNS

Cancer, epilepsy, diabetes, subluxating patellas, glaucoma, thyroid dysfunction, elbow and hip dysplasia (low incidence but seems to be on the increase).

DIANE LARATTA

SPECIAL COMMENTS

Sadly, cancer has a hold of this breed. Many don't live past seven years old. Discuss the prevalence of cancer with any breeder you consider.

ALSO SUITED FOR

Family Dog.

German Shorthaired Pointer

USUAL PLUSES

Always ready for anything. Here's a dog that, when mature, can run any distance you can, hike any trail, and generally keep up with whatever rigorous activity you enjoy. Handsome, loving dogs, their tails rarely stop wagging. Though generally friendly to people, they make serious watchdogs in their own home.

POSSIBLE DRAWBACKS

Temperaments range from unable to sit still for a minute to calm yet ready for anything. We prefer the latter. Be sure to meet at least the mother. If you wouldn't want to live with her, don't buy a puppy.

Since they were created to work independently, this breed does not hang on your every word like some herding dogs and retrievers. You will have to earn his respect with consistency, praise, and practice.

HEIGHT
21–25 inches.

WEIGHT
45–70 pounds.

COLOR

Brown and white, most have ticking—small brown spots all over the white.

GROOMING

Minimal. Regular ear care will be necessary.

SHEDDING

Moderate.

TRAINING

Mandatory. Early socialization and training will make all the difference. Some Shorthairs are overly protective of hearth and home. Others are not keen on strange animals of any kind. Early work can help prevent these problems by allowing you to direct the dog in positive ways if undesirable behavior develops.

EXERCISE

Mandatory. At least two off-lead romps in safe areas a day. Expect to spend 45 minutes or more each time. Ideally, find a few young dogs for him to play with. Nothing tires out a young dog like another young dog.

CHILDREN

Older children, with supervision. Shorthairs can be quite physical and can knock children over by mistake. Great playmates and usually tolerant of occasional painful mishap. A Shorthair in the right home with the right child(ren) is a great combination.

OTHER PETS

Usually good. Two males may have a hard time together and some Shorthairs are predatory, so they may not be good with cats. But if raised with other pets and trained properly, they should be fine.

BITE POTENTIAL

Low to moderate.

POSSIBLE HEALTH CONCERNS

Hip dysplasia, ear problems, and bloat.

SPECIAL COMMENTS

If you can give this breed the exercise and training he needs, he is a stalwart companion. Expect to crate your pup till up to two years of age to prevent bad habits from developing.

ALSO SUITED FOR

Watchdog.

LISEL DORESTE

Petit Basset Griffon Vendeen

USUAL PLUSES

PBGV is not only this breed's name, it could also be an acronym—Peppy, Busy, Gleeful, Vigorous. These adorable puppies grow up into playful, charming adults. Affectionate but not fawning, PBGVs keep busy smelling things, sight-seeing, or otherwise entertaining themselves. They have great senses of humor, so if you don't want a dog to make fun of you a bit, you might want to consider another breed.

POSSIBLE DRAWBACKS

Don't let their shape and the rubric "Basset" fool you—these animals have feisty blood coursing through their veins. Independent, self-assured, and prone to doing before thinking, their training needs to start early and continue. Be sure to stay positive, especially with the puppy training, as they do not respond well to harsh methods.

Can wander, have location-related deafness ("Gee, I'm far away from you so I don't hear you"), so keep him on-lead. Finds digging amusing. Howls and barks when bored, happy, lonely, frustrated, or excited.

HEIGHT
13–15 inches.

WEIGHT
35–45 pounds.

COLOR
White with lemon, orange, or grizzle (gray).

GROOMING
Minimal. This is a natural breed. A weekly brushing should do the trick. Regular ear care will be necessary.

SHEDDING
Minimal.

TRAINING
Mandatory, but make it fun and short. Unless taught early to respect you, he can grow up into an assertive, bossy dog.

EXERCISE

Mandatory. Active, active, active! These dogs are close to their hunting roots. Two decent romp/walk periods a day will keep him pretty much at a lope and off the countertops at home—most of the time.

CHILDREN

Generally good, but they won't always accept rough handling.

OTHER PETS

Careful! These are hunters and, unless taught otherwise, may annoy your cat.

BITE POTENTIAL

Low to moderate.

POSSIBLE HEALTH CONCERNS

Problems not common yet, but the ones cited are epilepsy, persistent pupillary membranes, aseptic meningitis, and flea allergy.

SPECIAL COMMENTS

Must be kept on-lead or in a fenced area. Never trust a Petit to return on your cue; he'll only return on his.

ALSO SUITED FOR

Watchdog.

SARAH WILSON

Siberian Husky

USUAL PLUSES

Playful, good-humored, with much joie de vivre, this is a breed for people who love having a dog to live with rather than have dominion over. Sibes are typically affectionate, happy dogs that want to be with you. If they are not adequately exercised or stimulated, their brightness can lead to boredom-related problems.

Normally friendly to people, this is not a breed prone to territorial aggression. They will occasionally bark or chortle to let you know someone is at the gate.

POSSIBLE DRAWBACKS

This can be a primitive breed—one that will dig, howl, or chew when bored or frustrated. Normally not a good nine-to-five dog. If not trained and managed properly, some will exhibit possessive, dominant, and predatory behaviors. Bred to keep moving, many will wander if given the opportunity, and few have a really reliable recall, especially when distracted. A securely fenced area is mandatory for safe play. Sibes are good at escaping, so don't leave them unattended for long.

HEIGHT
Under 23½ inches.

WEIGHT
35–60 pounds.

COLOR
Any.

GROOMING
Minimum. Not prone to tangles, though most dogs will enjoy a good weekly brushing.

SHEDDING
Sometime in the spring and sometime in the fall, your Sibe will shed. And shed. And shed. Hair will come out in clumps and handfuls. When she gets up off the rug, a thin mat of her own making will be left behind. You can survive this, armed with a vacuum, a good brush, and some determination. When you brush the dog (which ought to be twice a day at these times) you'll get so much hair you'll worry about bald spots—but there won't be any. There will just be more hair. When it is all over, you'll have your sleek, handsome, hardly-any-grooming-to-be-done dog back for another six months.

TRAINING

Professional assistance is mandatory. Start young and continue. These are bright dogs that love working as a team. A Siberian Husky will not, however, work as your slave. Engage them; do not try to subordinate them. Independent by design, off-leash control may be elusive.

EXERCISE

Triathlete. Daily romps and runs in fenced areas are mandatory. Walking on-lead is not enough.

CHILDREN

A guarded "fine" if raised with them. Some Sibes enjoy the company of children. Others are less tolerant. Select a calm, relaxed, easygoing puppy if you have children in your life.

OTHER PETS

Okay with other dogs of the same size or larger. Use caution with smaller animals of any species.

BITE POTENTIAL

Low to moderate.

POSSIBLE HEALTH CONCERNS

Eye problems are the most common. Some thyroid and epilepsy. Hip dysplasia does exist but is not yet prevalent.

SPECIAL COMMENTS

Though these dogs are highly adaptable, they do best in cooler climates.

ALSO SUITED FOR

Not for Everyone.

TONI KAY

Staffordshire Bull Terrier

USUAL PLUSES

One solid muscle, this dog has the body, heart, and brains to do almost any task you set for him. If you enjoy vim in your canine companion, a Staffy, who is active throughout his life, has it in buckets. People-loving by birth, this is a friendly, tail-thwacking, grinning, want-to-play dog.

POSSIBLE DRAWBACKS

In youth, their chewing prowess can be used for good (on toys of your choosing) or evil (you were ready to buy another couch anyway, weren't you?). Expect to spend money on toys, as they can take almost anything apart. Some Staffy folks simply give their dogs bowling balls to "play" with. Playing aggressive games with a Staffy puppy is stupid. It will encourage the wrong types of behaviors in this enthusiastic breed.

This power-packed dog was originally created for fighting. Breeders have worked hard to build on the breed's innate stability while minimizing its less desirable characteristics. Problems you can see are aggression toward other dogs (they may not pick a fight, but don't expect one to allow itself to be bullied), predatory behavior, and fence breaching (either by climbing, digging, or disassembly).

HEIGHT
14–16 inches.

WEIGHT
24–38 pounds.

COLOR
Anything goes, except black and tan and liver-colored.

GROOMING
Minimal.

SHEDDING
Minimal to moderate.

TRAINING
Professional assistance is mandatory. Start young and continue. Early on, convince the pup that you are a sane leader worth following, then never let him think anything different.

EXERCISE

Mandatory—securely fenced area only. Staffordshire Bull Terriers go like rockets. Expect two 30-to-45-minute games of ball a day to take the edge off.

CHILDREN

Usually excellent—patient and tolerant. Would not allow this breed, or any terrier or herding breed, to be loose outside with a bunch of squealing four-year-olds. Excited dogs make mistakes. Would not allow the child to get the dog "worked up" in play.

OTHER PETS

Usually fine, but avoid mixing same-sex dogs in the same household. Neutering is absolutely necessary.

MARUZELLA DELAGARZA

BITE POTENTIAL

Low to high. Once stimulated, some of these dogs can be highly predatory. Firm on-lead control and correct supervision will bring out the best in these fine dogs.

POSSIBLE HEALTH CONCERNS

This is a generally healthy breed. A few problems do exist. These include elongated palate, epilepsy, and cataracts. These dogs can overheat in hot weather.

SPECIAL COMMENTS

The "pit"-type dogs are getting a lot of bad press. If you elect to have a Staff Bull, do your part to change people's minds about this fine breed. Train her well, teach her cute tricks, socialize her with all kinds of people, and supervise her so she will be an ambassador for her breed. Be aware, though, that others may perceive even a minor breach in behavior as a big problem. Keep her on-lead or safely in fenced areas.

ALSO SUITED FOR

Watchdog, Not for Everyone.

Vizsla

USUAL PLUSES

This dog is a sweet, affectionate, trainable athlete. If you want a solid, russet, well-muscled canine that will curl up under the covers at night and run for hours by your side, a Vizsla is a good choice. Not as hardheaded as some of the other pointers, Vizslas are usually an easily trained breed.

POSSIBLE DRAWBACKS

The AKC standard for the Vizsla calls for "sensitive though fearless with a well-developed protective instinct." Although the description sounds great, it is actually a fairly hard combination to pull off. Combining sensitive and protective tendencies produces a dog prone to fear-based aggression. Sensibly, the AKC standard recognizes that possibility by advising owners: "Shyness, timidity or nervousness should be penalized." If you choose this lovely breed, please select a calm, confident pup. A Vizsla is not an easy choice for the city or as a nine-to-five dog, as they can chew, bark, or generally get into trouble if bored or underexercised.

A Vizsla can be overprotective of family or of "his" possessions. Can be aggressive toward other dogs, but not frequently. Some are sensitive to sudden sounds. Many are highly aware of visual stimulus, making them distractible. Some are shy with strangers.

HEIGHT
21–24 inches.

WEIGHT
Around 40–50 pounds.

COLOR
Golden rust.

GROOMING
Minimal brushing, but ears will need attention. Ask your breeder or vet for ear-care instructions if you aren't sure what to do.

SHEDDING
Minimal.

TRAINING

Mandatory. Start young and keep at it. Use positive, sensible methods that communicate your desires without frightening or hurting the dog. Work particularly on coming when called and developing good response to any command in distracting circumstances.

EXERCISE

Mandatory. Free runs twice daily in a fenced area will keep your Vizsla content. If he can play with another dog during his romps, he will be ecstatic!

CHILDREN

Good choice for older kids—if the dog is supervised, exercised, and taught appropriate behaviors.

OTHER PETS

Normally fine. Some Vizslas may be predatory, others aggressive toward other dogs, so select and train accordingly.

BITE POTENTIAL

Low to moderate.

POSSIBLE HEALTH CONCERNS

Hip dysplasia—though not a lot. Scbaccous andcnitis is also seen, though it's rare at this time.

SPECIAL COMMENTS

Brian's first dog, the beloved T, was a Vizsla. We both enjoy this breed, but it isn't the easiest dog to own. Exercise, socialization, and training will be a daily part of your life if you give your heart to a Vizsla.

ALSO SUITED FOR

Watchdog.

SARAH WILSON

Other high-input, high-output dogs are:

Airedale

Australian Shepherd

Border Collie

Chesapeake Bay Retriever

Doberman Pinscher

English Springer Spaniel

Newfoundland (kind of)

Norwegian Elkhound

Portuguese Water Dog

Rhodesian Ridgeback

Schipperke

Shiba Inu

Soft-Coated Wheaten Terrier

Standard Schnauzer

Tibetan Terrier

Welsh Springer Spaniel

Welsh Terrier

The City Dog

LANCE SMITH

The city dog is a companion animal that adapts well to the confines, noises, and activities of the average urban environment. This chapter contains only a small part of the possible list. If the owner takes responsibility for meeting its needs, almost any breed can thrive in the city. We would personally rather see dogs in the city than in the suburbs. Why? Because city dogs get more exercise, training, socialization, and interaction than many so-called country dogs. Every morning in most cities, groups of dog owners huddle over steaming cups of coffee. They don't know where the other people live or what they do; they know each other by their dogs. "Oh, here comes Buster's mom" is a common cry.

The dogs may romp with each other for an hour or so before trotting home. Many get walked midday for a half hour or more by a professional walker, a service offered in few suburban neighborhoods. There are even doggy day-care centers in many American cities. How many dogs in any other environment can claim this much fun? Add to this that nuisance behaviors, such as barking, must be addressed with training, not with isolation. Dogs need to have some semblance of manners or your daily walks will attract evil glares and nasty comments from others. That same social pressure happens if the dog is dirty, matted, or poorly cared for. Common problems people with city dogs address are eating off the sidewalk, aggression toward other dogs, barking, separation anxiety, heightened territoriality, pulling on-lead, jumping up, nuisance barking, and fashion faux pas (which occurs when a dog's collar doesn't match his new sweater).

Basset Hound

COMMON PLUSES

These are some of the cutest puppies — big-eared, big-pawed, sweet-breathed little houndlets. Usually happy and easygoing, Bassets make tail-thumping family companions that are not given to nuisance barking, territorial aggression, or hyperactivity. People who love them cite them as adaptable, eager to please (if properly motivated, i.e., with food), independent, and versatile.

POSSIBLE DRAWBACKS

May be difficult to housebreak. Many will howl when excited, bored, lonely, or happy. These hounds are consummate foodaholics, elevating begging to an art form. Some are possessive of toys and food. Although pack hounds normally get along well with other dogs, when Bassets don't, they really don't. Can have a musty, "houndy" smell. Regular ear cleaning is usually required.

HEIGHT
Around 14–15 inches.

WEIGHT
40–55 pounds.

COLOR

Any "hound" color, which seems to mean white with either black, tan, or lemon, or a combination of the three.

GROOMING

Minimal, though those ears need regular attention. Handling exercises done early and regularly will teach them to accept nail-cutting calmly. Some Bassets get extremely upset about pedicures.

SHEDDING

Minimal to moderate.

TRAINING

A good idea. "Leave it," "Out," and "Come" are mandatory, but don't trust your Basset. Once his nose starts working, his hearing seems to stop. Food is one of his great loves and is thus a powerful training tool. Most do not appreciate or respond well to harsh corrections.

EXERCISE

This is a big dog on short legs. If she isn't exercised regularly a Basset is prone to being overweight.

CHILDREN

Okay, but may not tolerate endless mauling, even if the child is friendly and well intentioned. Stick with kids who are past the ride-the-dog phase.

OTHER PETS

Normally fine, especially if raised with them. Some Bassets can be amazingly tough in a fight and don't always like canine company of the same sex.

BITE POTENTIAL

Normally low.

HEALTH CONCERNS

Ear infections, back problems, panosteitis, and bloat are the top problems. Some eye problems and bleeding disorders are lurking about, so look for tested parents.

SPECIAL COMMENTS

Crate-train and keep to schedule—housebreaking can be a challenge. Keep your Basset trim. Fat dogs are generally unhealthy, but letting a dog with a long back become overweight is sentencing him to painful, chronic health problems.

ALSO SUITED FOR

Good Dogs That Are Hard to Find.

MARY ANN SVIZENY

Boston Terrier

USUAL PLUSES

Nice compact, playful, affectionate, devoted little dogs that are one of the few breeds "Made in America." These guys are great fun, whether chasing a ball or going for a long walk. They have a jaunty self-importance about them that gives them an "I've got places to go and things to do" air. Affectionate without being fawning. Bostons are adaptable, easy-to-love companions.

POSSIBLE DRAWBACKS

Some Bostons can be barky, aggressive toward other dogs, and hard to housebreak. Their shortened face makes them prone to problems in the heat, as well as to snoring, grunting, and passing gas. It also means that their jaws and/or teeth can be deformed, leaving some Bostons unable to keep their tongue in their mouth. Some are high-strung, making early socialization and training a must.

HEIGHT

12–14 inches, give or take.

WEIGHT

Ranges from under 15 pounds up to 25 pounds.

COLOR

Brindle and white, black and white.

GROOMING

Minimal, but pay attention to facial folds during the summer.

SHEDDING

Minimal.

TRAINING

A good idea. Don't use slip collars with these dogs, as they can have tracheal sensitivity. Use a harness, a buckle collar, or, if something stronger is needed, a small prong collar.

EXERCISE

Daily, but a good fetch session in a long hall can suffice.

CHILDREN

Usually good, especially if raised with them and protected from rambunctious children. The Boston's protruding eyes are vulnerable to toddler-related mishaps.

OTHER PETS

Usually good. Males can fight if the same age or both are intact.

BITE POTENTIAL

Low.

HEALTH CONCERNS

Epilepsy, dental problems, sensitivity to heat, eye injury due to protruding eye placement.

SPECIAL COMMENTS

Again, their protruding eyes need protection. Be careful in heavy brush or weeds.

ALSO SUITED FOR

Watchdog.

TONI KAY

Bullmastiff

USUAL PLUSES

This huge dog, in the city? Surprisingly, they adapt quite well. Many of the giant breeds do better in the city than the midsized, but more active, retrievers. Bullmastiffs are fine, muscle-bound companions. Calm, kind, sensible—this is a pretty good choice for people who simply must have a huge dog. Generally good with good children.

Bred to knock down and detain their human quarry, they are not notorious biters. That's not to say they never would, but I know that most of these dogs are more inclined to sit on a person than to bite him. Nonetheless, being sat on makes a heck of an impression.

POSSIBLE DRAWBACKS

Their size makes even minor, "normal" behaviors like jumping up and pulling on-lead serious threats to human well-being. Because of this, training from puppyhood on is essential. Verbal control must be established early and maintained for the life of these dogs.

As for all giant dogs, health complaints such as short life, bloat, and cancer are a given. They also suffer from the short-nosed dog complaints of heat intolerance, snoring, and passing gas. Some Bullmastiffs drool. This is more of a problem for the males because of their larger heads. One shake of the head will spatter drool in all directions. Last, in the city, where all dog owners must pick up after their dogs, consider how you might do that. It is no small task.

HEIGHT
24–27 inches.

WEIGHT
100–130 pounds; some much larger.

COLOR
Fawn, red, brindle.

GROOMING
Minimal, though you may want to keep towels in strategic locations to wipe the drool off their mouths.

SHEDDING
Moderate.

TRAINING
Professional assistance is mandatory. Not because they are so difficult, but because they are so darn powerful. Verbal control is your only hope. Start them young, keep going, and you'll never be sorry. No rough games; he does not ever have to learn about aggression.

EXERCISE
Mandatory for their health, though they may try to talk you out of it. Not good in heat, so walks must be in the cool parts of the day.

PETER FERNANDEZ

CHILDREN
Good. Usually tolerant dogs, but as with all dog/child interactions, supervision and prevention of problems are a must.

OTHER PETS
Usually good when raised with other animals. Despite this, we would not house two intact males together, nor two dogs of the same age. If a Bullmastiff is aggressive, you are in serious trouble. Seek professional help instantly—this is not something you attempt to fix yourself

BITE POTENTIAL
Moderate. Not usually biters, but their size boosts them into the moderate category. They must be taken seriously.

HEALTH CONCERNS
Entropion, bloat, cancer, and hip dysplasia. Giant breeds do not live long, as a rule. It is as sad and simple as that.

SPECIAL COMMENTS
Real people-loving dogs, those big, thick, bratwurst tails never seem to stop wagging.

ALSO SUITED FOR
Nine-to-Five Dog, Family Dog, Not for Everyone.

Cardigan Welsh Corgi

USUAL PLUSES

Unusual-looking, devoted dogs that have the intelligence and character to do anything you want. Don't mistake those short legs for being clumsy; these dogs are vigorous and athletic. Playful with those they love, stoic and serious when necessary, these are interesting companions.

POSSIBLE DRAWBACKS

Cardigans are known for being a bit more standoffish and assertive than their cousin the Pembroke. Both these closely related breeds are cattle dogs, so they can be heel-nippers and pushy if not properly directed. Earning and keeping these dogs' respect is mandatory, but not especially difficult. Can bark if excited, bored, or suspicious. Digging is a favored hobby.

As a puppy, do not allow him to leap on and off of furniture. His long back and unusual front legs can be injured.

HEIGHT
10½–12½ inches.

WEIGHT
25–38 pounds

COLOR

Red, sable, brindle, black, or merle with white markings.

GROOMING

Minimal.

SHEDDING

Moderate.

TRAINING

Absolutely. This is a hardworking herding breed that needs activity and direction to be happy. Play fetch, train for agility, anything you like—but work him! He's worth it.

EXERCISE

Suggested. This is an active but adaptable breed that enjoys just about anything, whether going for a hike or playing couch potato in front of the TV. Enjoys plenty of exercise, but normally can skip a day or two here and there if he must.

CHILDREN

Best with older, supervised children.

OTHER PETS

Fine, especially if raised with them.

BITE POTENTIAL

Low to moderate.

POSSIBLE HEALTH CONCERNS

Generally healthy and long-lived. Can have eye problems, so buy from CERF'd parents.

SPECIAL COMMENTS

As of this writing, their numbers are on the rise, which bears watching. Though still a long way from popular (ranking 88th in a field of 145 in the 1997 statistics), their numbers have risen over 20 percent in a three-year period. This is a big jump for a breed with historically small numbers. If this trend continues, you may need to be vigilant in your selection of a Cardigan.

ALSO SUITED FOR

Watchdog.

CHRISTINE M. PELLICANO

Standard Dachshund

USUAL PLUSES

Have no fear if your Dachshund is near. Doxies have the answer to many of life's questions. What's the meaning of life? To play with me, of course! What is your life goal? To make me happy, of course! Is there a God? (I don't know for sure, but if there is, he has a Dachshund at his feet.) These playful, impish little dogs demand your attention, time, and heart. They insist on being involved with everything in your life. Inquisitive and smart, don't expect them to allow anything to happen in their home without their involvement.

Dachshunds come in three coat varieties—Smooth, Wirehaired, and Long-haired—and two sizes, Standard and Miniature. Rumor is that the Longhairs are the sweetest due to the spaniel genes introduced for the longer hair way back in the breeding process.

POSSIBLE DRAWBACKS

Dachshunds can be independent-minded, so work hard on your "Come" and "Leave it" commands. Once stimulated, don't expect them to hear you or respond. They live to chase squirrels. In the city, a drawback is a tendency to bark.

Be consistent with housebreaking, as they can be a bit creative in this area. Strict routine and supervision for the first six months is a good idea.

Some are surprisingly tough dogs. Snappishness, possessive aggression, and aggression toward other dogs are not unheard of.

HEIGHT
Approximately 9 inches.

WEIGHT
16–32 pounds.

COLOR
Most commonly black and tan or solid red, but can also be dappled (gray, white, tan, and black all mixed together).

GROOMING
Minimal.

SHEDDING
Minimal.

TRAINING

Mandatory. Early training and socialization will bring out the best in these intelligent dogs. Can develop aggression problems with other dogs. Can be snappy when held. Don't baby Dachshunds.

EXERCISE

Mandatory. Long, brisk walks do the trick.

CHILDREN

Older, calm children can be okay. Most Doxies do not like rough handling, and their long backs make them prone to injury. Once hurt, they never forget.

OTHER PETS

Best with dogs of the opposite sex. Can chase smaller animals or cats.

CHRISTINE M. PELLICANO

BITE POTENTIAL

Moderate. Can snap if physically harmed, frightened, or spoiled.

HEALTH CONCERNS

Your biggest worry is back injury, so prevent them from leaping on and off furniture and keep them slim. Other problems include eye disease, diabetes, and urinary-tract problems.

SPECIAL COMMENTS

Socialize early and do not reward barking, for this breed will kick up a fuss if he is encouraged to do so. Nevertheless, Doxies are usually sweet dogs, many of whom are big lickers.

ALSO SUITED FOR

Watchdog, Good Dogs That Are Hard to Find.

Norwich Terrier/Norfolk Terrier

USUAL PLUSES

First, let me apologize to all the Norfolk lovers out there who are probably darn tired of being paired for eternity with the Norwich. The fact is, however, that these dogs used to be considered two varieties of the same breed and only recently, in dog-breeding terms, were separated. Both breeds are wonderful—the Norfolk is not supposed to show any aggression and has folded ears. (NorFOLks have FOLds.) So, in theory, the Norfolk is a tiny bit sweeter than the Norwich, but that's like comparing honey to maple syrup.

Don't get us started on these dogs! They are way too cute: As puppies they are little wire-coated hedgehogs.

Playful, romping, mischievous, adorable little dogs, they love people and do not thrive in social isolation. Being a nine-to-five dog is hard on them unless you compensate with exercise and attention at either end of the day. Good town and country dogs for people with two homes.

POSSIBLE DRAWBACKS

Energetic, busy, squirrel chasers, hole diggers, Norwich/Norfolks must—must!—be kept on-lead or safely in a fenced yard. Can be barky, aggressive toward other dogs, and determined. They are, after all, terriers.

Early socialization is mandatory, as these guys can be nervous if they don't get out.

Because they tend to have difficulty breeding and produce small litters, the females may be coveted by breeders as future mothers. Prepare yourself for a high price and a wait for a pup, and to be happy with whatever sex/color you get.

HEIGHT
Around 10 inches.

WEIGHT
Around 12 pounds.

COLOR
Red, black and tan, grizzle.

GROOMING
Moderate to minimal. Coat sheds dirt easily. Wash and wear.

SHEDDING

Minimal, especially with regular grooming.

TRAINING

Okay, why not?

EXERCISE

Moderate. Although small, they need a good run every few days to let off steam. As they mature, their exercise needs can be met by playing ball down a hall or in a small backyard.

CHILDREN

Don't let toddlers hurt them by mistake, but generally a good match for good kids.

OTHER PETS

Normally fine. May chase cats and may fight with dogs of the same sex.

BITE POTENTIAL

Low.

HEALTH CONCERNS

Epilepsy is the worst worry for a Norfolk/Norwich pet owner. Dental problems are commonplace, so at-home tooth care and veterinary attention twice a year is necessary. Breeders have to contend with a seeming myriad of reproductive challenges.

SARAH WILSON

SPECIAL COMMENTS

Neuter early (as soon as your veterinarian will do the surgery), as the males can be leg lifters. Watch their weight. They are effective beggers, but do not succumb to their charms.

ALSO SUITED FOR

Family Dog, Watchdog, Low-Shed Breed

Scottish Terrier

USUAL PLUSES

These are proud dogs that are devoted to their family and friends. They love to romp as puppies; a Scottie will wiggle up to you, charming you into a game. Very much one-person or one-family dogs, they are loyal to their last breath. Viewing the world with an unworried eye, a Scottie is a great traveler. For Scottie lovers, their independence is part of their charm. As one owner says, "I come home, he looks up from his basket. 'Oh,' he seems to say. 'It's you.' He just cracks me up!"

POSSIBLE DRAWBACKS

Because he can be so self-reliant, he generally takes his own counsel on what needs to be done and when. Obedience training should start early and continue. Choose a method that works with him, not against him. Do not play rough games with him; he is way too feisty for that. Some can be aggressive. For Scotties, size really doesn't matter. No dog is too big to take on. In his confident mind, the bigger they come, the harder they fall. The "terrier" at the end of his name means he may bark, chase, nip, and dig.

HEIGHT
Around 10 inches.

WEIGHT
18–22 pounds.

COLOR
Black, gray, brindle, wheaten.

GROOMING

Professional assistance is mandatory if you want him to look like a Scottie. Otherwise he will blossom into a moving dust-bunny in no time. Handling exercises throughout his life will help him learn to tolerate grooming politely.

SHEDDING
Minimal.

TRAINING

Mandatory. Early socialization and puppy training will bring out the most in your Scottie. He is always up for a game. If you add play to your training, you will achieve better results. You'll have to work on developing a good "Leave it" command, as once he is focused on something, responding to commands is not high on his list.

EXERCISE

Moderate. A few good games of fetch a day will do nicely. Keep him on a leash for his own safety. As a walking partner, hard to beat.

CHILDREN

Mature dogs with older kids may be fine. No aggressive games, and no childish teasing of the dog allowed—that goes for adults, too!

OTHER PETS

Can be okay if raised with the other pets. No smaller animals, please; these guys are apt to be predatory. Same-sex dogs may well fight each other. Unless socialized early, don't expect a Scottie to be thrilled with other dogs in his home.

BITE POTENTIAL

Average to high.

M. MᶜGHEE

POSSIBLE HEALTH CONCERNS

Von Willebrand's disease (there is now an accurate genetic test for vWD, which all breeders should be using), Scottie cramp. Dental problems are commonplace, so regular at-home tooth care and veterinary attention is called for.

SPECIAL COMMENTS

Can be particularly sensitive to fleas.

ALSO SUITED FOR

Low-Shed Breed, Watchdog.

Shiba Inu

USUAL PLUSES

Foxlike in body, quick in thought, this is a frighteningly smart dog in a charming little package. Naturally clean, normally quiet, this breed's numbers are up. In 1993 they ranked 81st with the AKC but by 1997 they were 64th. With their adorable looks, it is easy to see why their star is rising.

POSSIBLE DRAWBACKS

Do not confuse smart with willing to please. Shibas are independent dogs that tend to take things into their own paws. Skilled at games such as keep-away, they will lead you on a chase over couch and coffee table with lightning speed and a merry Shiba grin. Not likely to obey for the sake of obeying. Males can be aggressive toward other dogs. Neuter males early (no later than six months of age) to prevent leg-lifting and macho tendencies. Aloof with strangers, self-contained in general, bold as brass, and always impressed with himself, this is not the stuffed toy he appears to be. When thwarted, a Shiba can scream! Be forewarned: It is a memorable sound.

HEIGHT
13½–16½ inches.

WEIGHT
Approximately 25 pounds.

COLOR
All colors acceptable, but red, sesame, and black and tan are most common.

GROOMING
Minimal. A natural breed that needs only an occasional brushing to keep them looking up to snuff.

SHEDDING
Usually average. A lot when that thick coat sheds out twice a year.

TRAINING
Mandatory. Plenty bright; your job is to find some way to engage that mind. Too much force is likely to be met with both disdain and resistance. Start early, socialize extensively, get guidance from experienced people, and never trust your Shiba off-lead.

EXERCISE

Mandatory. This active breed gets quite a bit of exercise careening around your home. But if you would prefer he did not do that, then a couple of long walks a day (½ mile or more each) will help. Shibas are gravity-defying creatures that'll derive endless pleasure from playing with canine friends.

CHILDREN

Older, calm children with older, calm dogs. Shibas are generally not fans of being chased, hugged too hard, or manhandled. Most will try to retreat, but if retreat is impossible, they may protect themselves.

OTHER PETS

Okay if raised with them. Would not mix two intact males, especially of a similar age. Would not mix a Shiba, hunting dog that he is, with small pets.

BITE POTENTIAL

Average, unless they are being forced in some way, then some may bite. Early handling helps prevent this.

LANCE SMITH

POSSIBLE HEALTH CONCERNS

Generally a healthy breed at this point. Some subluxating patellas, a bit of hip dysplasia, but not much. Skin and eyes are fundamentally healthy but buy from CERF'd parents anyway.

SPECIAL COMMENTS

Pups are very active, inquisitive, and oral. You will have to supervise him closely to keep him out of trouble. Buy a crate and use it.

Containment is mandatory. Agile, they are fence scalers and tunnel builders, so don't leave your Shiba unsupervised, even in a fenced area. A kennel run with both a secure top and a dig-resistant flooring is the only safe kind.

ALSO SUITED FOR

High-Input, High-Output Dog.

Tibetan Terrier

USUAL PLUSES

TTs are happy sprites. Bouncy, fun-filled, and affectionate, these imps are not above making mischief. These dogs want and demand your attention. Bored Tibetans make all kinds of inconvenient discoveries, from how to open their crate to how to get into a cabinet. This is utterly charming if you enjoy that kind of precociousness, and endlessly frustrating if you don't.

POSSIBLE DRAWBACKS

Considered by some too active, demanding, and naughty to be a good match with either the oldest or the youngest in our midst. This breed does not mature quickly mentally and will need puppy supervision, direction, and entertainment longer than most breeds. Some can be shy with strangers, others can become possessive. If you glimpse either of these traits, cut them off at the pass with help from an experienced trainer.

HEIGHT
14–16 inches.

WEIGHT
18–30 pounds.

COLOR
Any.

GROOMING
Thorough brushing two to three times a week.

SHEDDING
Moderate.

TRAINING
Recommended. Find a teacher who enjoys and uses creativity in teaching. Endless repetition will bore your Tibetan. Engage their mind; you won't be able to bridle their spirit.

EXERCISE

Recommended. This is a lively dog; indoor play goes a long way, but outdoor romps in safe areas and long walks are always appreciated.

CHILDREN

Generally okay. Older, calm children best. Can become mouthy when overexcited, as almost all dogs can. Do not allow unsupervised roughhousing. Some can be possessive of objects around children.

OTHER PETS

Generally okay, especially when raised with other animals. TTs are generally gregarious dogs.

BITE POTENTIAL

Low with proper selection, training, and management.

HEALTH CONCERNS

Generally healthy. Responsible breeders CERF and OFA their dogs to monitor any developing problems.

SPECIAL COMMENTS

Be vigilant about housebreaking, as TTs can get into bad habits easily. Supervision, routine, and confinement are key.

ALSO SUITED FOR

High-Input, High-Output Dog; Watchdog; Low-Shed Breed.

LINDA ROSA

Welsh Terrier

USUAL PLUSES

Welshies are inquisitive, alert, and trainable. Though they will not back down if challenged, they are not quite as pugnacious as some other terrier breeds. Positively dapper when groomed professionally, this is a clean, appealing companion dog.

POSSIBLE DRAWBACKS

Welshies are terriers, so some are hard to control when stimulated. Keep him on-lead unless the area is safely fenced. They can also be diggers, predatory, and aggressive toward strange dogs, especially of the same sex. Early socialization and training help prevent these problems from developing.

HEIGHT
14½–15½ inches.

WEIGHT
About 18–20 pounds.

COLOR
Black and tan, black grizzle and tan.

GROOMING
Professional grooming is mandatory. Take these dogs to a groomer every other month.

SHEDDING
Minimal.

TRAINING
Mandatory. Critical commands are "Come," "Leave it," and "Down." Puppies benefit greatly from the early training and socialization offered in puppy kindergarten classes.

EXERCISE
Mandatory. Indoor play is not sufficient. A couple of brisk walks a day of half a mile or more, along with a lively game or two of fetch, will take the edge off of most Welshies.

CHILDREN

Well-trained and supervised adult dogs with well-mannered, older children is best.

OTHER PETS

Another dog of a different age and sex should be fine. Acceptance of cats varies, from playmate to plaything.

BITE POTENTIAL

Low to high. Isn't likely to tolerate endless childish mauling. Early handling exercises vital.

HEALTH CONCERNS

Generally healthy at this point. Some skin issues and eye problems do occur, but they are rare.

SPECIAL COMMENTS

Neutering males early (under six months) can prevent problems such as leg lifting and overassertiveness. This is one of the rarer breeds we recommend; be prepared to wait for a puppy.

ALSO SUITED FOR

Low-Shed Breed; High-Input, High-Output Dog; Watchdog.

D. SCOTT LUNSFORD

Other breeds to consider for the city are:

American Cocker Spaniel

Australian Terrier

Bichon Frise

Cairn Terrier

Cavalier King Charles Spaniel

Chihuahua

Chinese Crested

Dachshund (Miniature)

English Cocker Spaniel

French Bulldog

Italian Greyhound

Japanese Chin

Keeshond

Maltese

Miniature Pinscher

Miniature Schnauzer

Papillon

Pekingese

Pomeranian

Pug

Shih Tzu

Silky Terrier

West Highland White Terrier

Whippet

Yorkshire Terrier

Virtually any breed can be successfully owned in the city. If you run eight miles a day in the park, a Weimaraner will work well for you. If you do not, a Weim would be an extraordinarily poor choice. The dogs listed above are dogs that can adapt to urban life with the least stress on them and, hence, on you.

CHRISTINE M. PELLICANO

The Indoor Companion

These charming animals are for people who need a strictly indoor companion. Because of rather obvious hygiene issues, these dogs must be small in size. This does not imply that other dogs don't make wonderful calm indoor companions, just that larger dogs need access to the outside.

All dogs benefit from outdoor jaunts, but for the dogs listed here, such jaunts are additions to their life, not day-to-day necessities. However, just because these dogs

CHRISTINE M. PELLICANO

can adapt well to an indoor life doesn't mean they are limited to it. Many of these breeds are terrific all-round dogs.

Here are a few general considerations for the potential small-dog owner:

HOUSEBREAKING – Many of these breeds are notorious for being difficult to housebreak. This is largely an owner-caused problem, which can be eliminated (if you pardon the pun) by serious supervision and early training. In general, females are easier to paper-train than males.

LEG LIFTING – This is a common problem, largely preventable with early neutering and training.

LARGER DOGS – As gregarious as your toy dog may be, allowing her to play with larger dogs is asking for trouble. A friendly swipe from a Labrador paw can seriously injure a toy dog.

SMALL CHILDREN – Dogs squirm, small children drop—this is not a mix that we recommend. Toy breeds are too easy to injure and too prone to becoming fearful or aggressive after injury. Who can blame them? If you aren't going to protect them, who will?

NASTY WEATHER – Toys get cold more easily than their larger counterparts. They should not be subjected to cold or wet and should have outerwear if they go out in inclement weather.

LEG BREAKS – Fearless is a good description of many toys. They leap off of couches onto hardwood floors without a second thought, a feat roughly equivalent to you leaping off the roof of your house onto greased concrete. Pups in particular can make dangerous decisions. Do not encourage leaping. Teach them to use ramps or to hop from the couch to a stool and then down.

CHRISTINE M. PELLICANO

ROSE MARCHETTI

Is Smaller Better?

Unusually tiny toys: Aren't they just adorable? Not to us. The tinier the dog the more prone they are to serious health and temperament problems. Just yesterday a three-pound Maltese died from diarrhea that would not have slowed down a Labrador.

Stay away from a "teacup" or "pocket" anything. Yes, they are precious, but they are also delicate and too often neurotic. People even have the nerve to sell these problems for a higher price! Get a "normal"-sized one. Even a largish Yorkie is a tiny dog.

CHRISTINE M. PELLICANO

Chihuahua

USUAL PLUSES

Chihuahuas are devoted, charming, bright dogs that will never leave your side. They have no greater dream in life than to be with you, so they are fine companions. Not especially hard to train, it is a shame to waste their brain. Teach them things; they enjoy pleasing you.

POSSIBLE DRAWBACKS

These are real snobs. Chihuahuas like their family, other Chihuahuas, and little else. Most are not friendly to strangers and can nip if you insist on making advances. Overly protective of "their" person, this can be a surprisingly intimidating little dog.

Because these guys are truly tiny, shyness is understandable, but it still needs to be worked on. Select a relaxed pup, then socialize him a great deal. Many are yappy.

HEIGHT
Around 5 inches.

WEIGHT
Under 6 pounds.

COLOR
Any.

GROOMING
Smooth-coated: Minimal. Long-coated: Moderate.

SHEDDING
Minimal for both.

TRAINING
Early socialization benefits this breed greatly. There is no reason that they should be frightened of the world. Wonderful little trick dogs, they are too cute performing any command.

EXERCISE
Minimal.

CHILDREN

No. Chis are too small and too opinionated.

OTHER PETS

Maybe—depends. Chihuahuas are very possessive of "their" person, so they can be aggressive to other animals they perceive as competition. They tend to enjoy the company of other Chihuahuas.

BITE POTENTIAL

Moderate with owners. Can be high with strangers and children.

MARY JANE DAVIS

POSSIBLE HEALTH CONCERNS

Subluxating patellas are the most common problem. OFA registration of the knee joint is now possible, so ask the breeder about that. Heart murmurs, dental problems, and collapsing trachea are also seen.

SPECIAL COMMENTS

Generally a healthy, long-lived breed, you can expect to enjoy their company for 15 or more years.

ALSO SUITED FOR

City Dog, Watchdog, Good Dogs That Are Hard to Find.

Training Tips for Toys

Many of these dogs are delicate, and prone to collapsing tracheas. Either use a harness or use the widest collar you can find. The wider the collar the more gentle it is on the neck. Do not pull straight up on the lead, as that can irritate the trachea.

Training methods that employ rough jerks on the neck can hurt a toy dog. Human rage can also cause injury, so stay calm. Teach with clear, gentle methods. Don't confuse firmness with meanness or follow through with anger. Don't be a pushover; just remember how small your dog is. No dog needs our rage, but with toys it can lead to real injury.

Italian Greyhound

USUAL PLUSES

These animals are exquisite little beauties. Sweet, affectionate, quiet, and devoted, if you want a companion that is clean, cheerful, and largely trouble-free, by all means look at this breed more closely.

Highly adaptable, they grace your city apartment and your country home with equal ease. Generally long-lived, it is not uncommon for them to live 15 years or more.

POSSIBLE DRAWBACKS

These guys need you, they crave you, they cannot live without you. They want to be with you, by you, and on you. If you are not interested in having an elegant shadow curled in a ball on your lap, dancing around your feet, or nestled under the covers, find another breed. These dogs were created to be companions and do that job well.

IGs need socialization and early training to moderate their natural tendency toward shyness. A few can be barky.

HEIGHT
13–15 inches.

WEIGHT
Around 10 pounds.

COLOR
Fawn, red, blue, black, and piebald (large patches of color on white).

GROOMING
Minimal.

SHEDDING
Minimal.

TRAINING
For fun; use positive methods that both you and the dog enjoy. They cannot tolerate harsh methods, physically or mentally.

EXERCISE

Always appreciated, but they get lots just running around the average home. Let them off-lead in fenced-in areas only, as these dogs will instantly chase small animals.

CHILDREN

Not normally. IGs do not enjoy loud noise or chaos—two things children specialize in.

OTHER PETS

Good, though larger dogs may intimidate or injure them. May give chase to the cats, but at ten pounds, IGs pose little danger.

BITE POTENTIAL

Usually low. May snap if they feel threatened.

POSSIBLE HEALTH CONCERNS

Not many. Ask about epilepsy, subluxating patellas, and eye problems. Blues can have balding and skin problems.

SPECIAL COMMENTS

These dogs need outerwear in rain or cold. Be careful with flea and tick products and other chemicals; these little guys can be quite sensitive. Ask your veterinarian or breeder what she or he recommends.

ALSO SUITED FOR

City Dog.

JULIE SHEEHAN

Japanese Chin

USUAL PLUSES

Elegant, self-possessed little dogs. Delightful companions that blend into your life with ease. In general, these dogs are not yappers, though they will certainly alert you when someone is at the door. Small, sweet, calm, beautiful—these dogs are a joy to travel with and a pleasure to own.

Generally long-lived. You can hope for about 15 years from your companion.

POSSIBLE DRAWBACKS

Short-faced, so expect the usual snorting, snoring, gas, and heat sensitivity. Can be a bit independent, and sometimes stubborn, but neither is a major flaw.

HEIGHT

8–10 inches.

WEIGHT

Around 7 pounds.

COLOR

White with patches of color. Patch color includes black, red, brindle, and lemon.

GROOMING

Moderate.

SHEDDING

More than you might think.

TRAINING

Why not? Use positive methods, as these little sweethearts will not comprehend anger or meanness.

EXERCISE

Minimal.

CHILDREN

Okay for older children.

OTHER PETS

Good, though not safe with much larger dogs.

BITE POTENTIAL

Low.

POSSIBLE HEALTH CONCERNS

Subluxating patellas, entropion. Eye injury and heat sensitivity are your biggest concerns.

SPECIAL COMMENTS

Chin lovers are smitten by their breed. No other group responded to our requests for photos with the overwhelming enthusiasm of Chin folk. They think there is something very special about their dogs and, judging from their reaction, we have to agree.

ROSE MARCHETTI

ALSO SUITED FOR

City Dog, Nine-to-Five Dog.

Maltese

USUAL PLUSES

Sarah lost her heart to a Maltese we were training and now is utterly useless around these dogs. These bright, bright, bright little creatures are agile, playful, bold, and convinced that everyone in the world is just waiting to meet them! Highly trainable, as long as you don't allow them to believe they rule the world.

POSSIBLE DRAWBACKS

Can be barky, hard to housebreak, unresponsive to commands, and overly protective, but all of these are owner-caused problems. Get them as pups, treat them like dogs, hide your amusement at their cute but naughty behaviors, and expect greatness; this is a breed that can deliver on that expectation. Leg lifting and aggressive behavior can be problems if you spoil them.

HEIGHT
8 inches.

WEIGHT
Under 7 pounds.

COLOR
White.

GROOMING

Professional attention is required. We recommend keeping them clipped down. Not only is this easier for both of you, but on a Maltese it is just too cute for words.

SHEDDING
Minimal.

TRAINING
Recommended. If you do not train a Maltese, he will surely train you!

EXERCISE
Recommended, though daily indoor play will do the trick for many.

CHILDREN
Usually fine with older, careful children.

OTHER PETS

Normally good, though be careful around larger dogs.

BITE POTENTIAL

Low to high.

POSSIBLE HEALTH CONCERNS

Subluxating patellas, tear staining (brown discoloration under the eye), eye infections, dental problems, and hypoglycemia.

SPECIAL COMMENTS

Buy a large Maltese, as the tiny ones are more problem-prone in every way. If you use a collar on these dogs, choose a *wide* one, as a narrow one will be harder on the dog's neck.

ALSO SUITED FOR

City Dog, Watchdog, Good Dogs That Are Hard to Find.

CHRISTINE M. PELLICANO

Miniature Dachshund

USUAL PLUSES

These little joys range from playful and silly to strong-minded and determined. A Miniature does not consider himself small in the least, and he does not require coddling. Inquisitive and bold by nature, this little dog will go anywhere and try and do anything.

POSSIBLE DRAWBACKS

Can be barky. They are fabulous diggers and quite the escape artists. Can develop aggressive behavior.

   Like all long-backed breeds, prone to back problems. Limit leaping on and off of furniture because of this. A couple of carpeted ramps or a lower cushion to hop up and down on can help.

HEIGHT

About 5 inches.

WEIGHT

Under 11 pounds.

COLOR

Most commonly solid red, but can be solid cream. Also black, red, fawn, brown, or gray with tan points. There is also a dappled color.

GROOMING

Varies with the coat type, but minimal for the Smooth and moderate for the Long- and Wirehaired.

SHEDDING

Varies—minimal to moderate.

TRAINING

Mandatory for the mental health of this bright little dog. For these impulsive dogs, command training is necessary for safety's sake. Find a trainer who makes training fun for both you and the dog. Dachshunds are highly trainable if you include them and can be highly resistant if you hurt or frighten them.

EXERCISE

Necessary, but their size makes indoor exercise easy.

CHILDREN

Good with well-behaved children but can snap if they are consistently hurt or threatened.

OTHER PETS

Usually good if raised with them. Can be aggressive toward strange dogs. Larger dogs can inadvertently injure a small Doxie.

BITE POTENTIAL

Medium, unless hurt, threatened, or allowed to rule the roost.

CHRISTINE M. PELLICANO

POSSIBLE HEALTH CONCERNS

A variety of eye disorders, so CERF parents are important. Back problems come with the territory. Some problems with epilepsy, kidney function, diabetes, and deafness.

SPECIAL COMMENTS

These dogs have been popular for decades, so be picky; a good example of this breed will give you years of joy. We are especially fond of the Longhair Doxies.

ALSO SUITED FOR

City Dog, Watchdog, Good Dogs That Are Hard to Find.

Papillon

USUAL PLUSES

Expect a bonded, devoted, stable, bright companion that will respond with a canine "Yes, I can!" to anything you have in mind. Highly trainable and eager to please, many of these dynamos compete at the highest level of obedience and agility competition. We are both fans of the adaptable, sweet, and pretty "Pap."

POSSIBLE DRAWBACKS

Socialize early, as shyness can develop. If this behavior is encouraged, Paps can become shaking little weenies. This is not what the breed is or should be. Treat them like the confident, bold little dogs they were born to be and you will have a knockout companion dog.

Housebreaking needs to be taken seriously. Can be quite barky.

HEIGHT
8–11 inches.

WEIGHT
Around 8–10 pounds.

COLOR
White with patches of color.

GROOMING
As needed. Usually twice a week does the trick.

SHEDDING
Minimal to moderate.

TRAINING
Absolutely! Too much fun for man and beast to skip this. One of the quintessential trick dogs. Paps are easy to train and eager to please.

EXERCISE
Moderate, though always appreciated.

CHILDREN
Fine for older, careful children.

OTHER PETS

Fine, as far as the Pap is concerned.

BITE POTENTIAL

Low.

POSSIBLE HEALTH CONCERNS

Not many. Subluxating patellas are your biggest concern. OFA now certifies knees, so look for that, or at least veterinary confirmation that both parents are sound.

SPECIAL COMMENTS

Neuter males early to prevent leg-lifting habits from developing. Paps are versatile dogs that enjoy all kinds of activities.

ALSO SUITED FOR

City Dog, Watchdog.

DIANA GONZALEZ

Yorkshire Terrier

USUAL PLUSES

Prepare to be smitten. A tiny little head cock from a petite pup with an "I have arrived" attitude is enough to fell many a human. Devoted to their people, this is an excellent companion animal.

Love them dearly but treat them like real dogs, and a real dog you will have. Spoil them like baby dolls and you will create a shy, quaking, yappy brat-dog.

POSSIBLE DRAWBACKS

Assertive, bold, barky, determined—this very small dog body contains a very big dog spirit. Their size makes them easy to spoil; their soul renders them charming tyrants. Can be the ultimate brat: aggressive, haughty, naughty, and downright disobedient.

HEIGHT
Around 7–9 inches.

WEIGHT
3–7 pounds.

COLOR

Gray and tan as adults. Yorkies start out darker and lighten with age.

GROOMING

Professional grooming is mandatory. Pet clip recommended. Toy breeds tend to develop tartar, so regular dental care is necessary.

SHEDDING
Minimal.

TRAINING

Professional assistance is suggested. Bright, assertive, bold, and born to be spoiled, this little dog deserves all the education he can get. Don't fight with him; he has grit. Choose another breed if you lose your temper—these little ones can get hurt. Do teach him; he will learn and learn and learn.

EXERCISE

Mandatory. These are active dogs, though indoor activity can suffice. Keep on-lead around larger dogs, as most Yorkies will not hesitate to challenge a Great Dane.

CHILDREN

Not usually. If hurt, threatened, or allowed to believe they are in charge (a common Yorkie conviction), they will snap.

OTHER PETS

Caution. Big spirit–small package combo can lead to injury by larger dogs—and almost everyone is larger. Can harass cats.

BITE POTENTIAL

Moderate to high.

POSSIBLE HEALTH CONCERNS

Subluxating patellas, collapsing trachea, pancreatitis, hypoglycemia (especially in puppies and tiny adults), digestive complaints ranging from diarrhea to vomiting, liver shunt.

SPECIAL COMMENTS

Extremely popular breed; be selective about who you buy from. Please buy a normal-to-large-sized Yorkie. Generally long-lived, 15-plus is not unusual.

ALSO SUITED FOR

Watchdog, City Dog, Low-Shed Breed, Good Dogs That Are Hard to Find.

SARAH WILSON

Other breeds that are equally well suited as indoor companions:

Boston Terrier (Small)

Miniature Pinscher

Pekingese

Pomeranian

Pug

Shih Tzu

Silky Terrier

Toy Poodle

The Low-Shed Breeds

Here's a soup-to-nuts collection of dogs. Some are active and athletic, some are more demure and laid-back. The only common denominator is their low-shed status.

Please note: These dogs are low-shed, not no-shed. These are dogs that are normally classed as "hypoallergenic," but no dog is hypoallergenic to all people. Whether you or your child will tolerate the presence of a certain breed remains to be seen. Some people are allergic to hair, others dander, still a few more to saliva. The only way to determine if a dog is irritating to your allergies is to test-drive a few.

A few words of caution: Higher numbers of animals add to the allergy load. Normally animal-tolerant people can start sneezing the moment they walk into our house. We have five dogs and three cats living with us, and no matter how careful we are, dander and hair are everywhere. Visiting a breeder who has multiple dogs in the house may not give you a true view of your tolerance for that breed.

LAUREN McDERMOTT

Almost every breed in this lineup requires professional grooming four or more times a year. All will need weekly, or more frequent, brushing. The softer, cottony-coated dogs will need regular bathing. That is the downside to this group: You don't have to vacuum much, but that doesn't mean you won't be dealing with hair. You'll just have to cope with it on the dog instead of off.

With all this in mind, go out and find a dog! Chances are, if there is a breed out there that won't set you sneezing, it is in this chapter!

Airedale

USUAL PLUSES

Playful, fun-loving, smart, active—this versatile breed has the potential to do it all and then some. These dogs can be hunting companions, agility pros, search-and-rescue enthusiasts, and much more. They will be limited only by your limitations.

As a breed, they are protective of their family and home. This instinct to protect can be balanced with excellent verbal control and extensive socialization when young.

POSSIBLE DRAWBACKS

Active! Remember, this is one of the largest of the terrier breeds. This means they can be strong-willed, stoic, and generally unimpressed by human hysteria. Mental control needs to be established and maintained through positive, non-negotiable training that you apply every day, throughout the day. If you are unsure of yourself or inconsistent in your reinforcement, you're sunk.

Possible problems are fighting with other dogs, predatory behavior, jumping, barking, digging, chewing, possessiveness, and challenges to humans. These can usually be prevented or controlled through proper selection, management, and training.

HEIGHT

23 inches, plus or minus.

WEIGHT

Around 45–50 pounds.

COLOR

Black and tan.

GROOMING

Professional attention is mandatory, as least four times a year. Weekly brushing in between. Ignoring these needs allows your dapper Airedale to blossom into a woolly bison-shaped creature that neither looks nor smells especially attractive.

SHEDDING

None to light if properly groomed. If the coat is allowed to grow out, shedding can be a problem.

TRAINING

Professional assistance is mandatory. Start early and keep going. Though their gleeful youth can be trying, getting through it is well worth the effort.

EXERCISE

A lot. They'll take everything you give them and more, but they can manage on an hour or so a day in the city if they must.

CHILDREN

Good Airedales are good with good kids. Well-socialized, well-trained, and well-supervised Airedales can take rough-and-tumble games in stride, but do not expect teasing, taunting, or abuse to be tolerated.

OTHER PETS

Fine with animals they are raised with. Do not keep two male dogs of the same age. Males must be neutered.

BITE POTENTIAL

Moderate to high. This is very dependent on you.

COMMON HEALTH CONCERNS

Minimal reported: some cancer, some hypothyroidism, minimal hip dysplasia, some allergies, some itchy skin.

ANAHID JUOZAITIS

SPECIAL COMMENTS

Airedales are talented, bright dogs with much potential. How that potential is developed is wholly up to you. If you are ready for this dog, you will not be disappointed.

ALSO SUITED FOR

High-Input, High-Output Dog; Watchdog; Not for Everyone.

Australian Terrier

USUAL PLUSES

Alert, busy, playful, affectionate, this is a wonderful little dog. Happy when all is well, on his toes when duty calls, the Aussie is a great little companion. Aussies attach deeply to their people and want to please them. Not especially prone to aggression. Not as yappy as some other terriers.

POSSIBLE DRAWBACKS

Hobbies like digging or climbing on things are common. These dogs do not isolate well and do best with their people. Although he cares about pleasing you more than some other terriers, he will bolt if he sees something worth chasing. Keep him on-lead!

Typical terrier challenges, such as barking, small-animal chasing, digging, and aggression toward other dogs, can be present. Early socialization and training help to control these tendencies.

HEIGHT
10–11 inches.

WEIGHT
Around 12–16 pounds.

COLOR
Black and tan, or solid red.

GROOMING
Little.

SHEDDING
Minimal.

TRAINING

Excellent idea—your dog will love it. Work hard on "Come" and "Leave it." Those commands are your emergency brakes; never trust a terrier off-lead. Have fun! Repetition will cause boredom that will lead directly to creative canine response.

EXERCISE
Moderate. A good game of fetch in the backyard will do the trick.

CHILDREN

Generally good with good children. Do not allow taunting and rough-and-tumble play. Although he is fairly tolerant, he will not accept endless teasing; but then no one likes that.

OTHER PETS

Usually fine. Do not expect two males to live in harmony. All male companion dogs should be neutered to avoid leg lifting and attitude problems.

BITE POTENTIAL

Low, unless hurt, taunted, or teased.

SARAH WILSON

POSSIBLE HEALTH CONCERNS

Usually a healthy breed. Occasional diabetes, thyroid, and allergy problems, but these are not common. Some subluxating patellas and some Legg-Calves Perthes disease.

SPECIAL COMMENTS

A terrific breed that will no doubt garner more popularity than they presently enjoy.

ALSO SUITED FOR

City Dog, Watchdog.

Bichon Frise

USUAL PLUSES

Little cotton-candy dogs, Bichons are sweet, loving, and easy to live with. Generally friendly to all, a good Bichon is a canine ambassador.

Playful, eager to please, gentle, and craving human company, this wonderful companion dog adapts easily to many different lifestyles.

POSSIBLE DRAWBACKS

Can be hard to housebreak, so start young and be persistent. Neuter males early, as leg lifting can be a problem. Because of increasing popularity and attendant poor breeding practices, some shyness and, rarely, some aggression have cropped up. Take your time when looking for a breeder.

HEIGHT
9½–11½ inches.

WEIGHT
Around 7–12 pounds.

COLOR

White. Some have buff, cream, or apricot shading.

GROOMING

Professional grooming is mandatory—every month. Cottony coat tends to mat if not brushed thoroughly a couple of times a week. Mats seem to develop within minutes if the coat gets wet. Gets very dirty walking on city streets.

SHEDDING

None.

TRAINING

Yes. Wonderful trick dogs, they enjoy the interaction and attention positive training brings them.

EXERCISE

Yes. Needs more than an indoor romp to be calm and relaxed.

CHILDREN

Good match, though some are pain-sensitive, which means older, careful children only.

OTHER PETS

Yes. Plays well with others.

BITE POTENTIAL

Low to moderate.

POSSIBLE HEALTH CONCERNS

Subluxating patellas, epilepsy, tartar buildup on teeth, skin problems, flea allergy, bladder stones, disk problems, cataracts, tear staining.

SPECIAL COMMENTS

Find a gentle groomer, then see her regularly. Grooming out a matted dog is painful for the dog, and Bichons will resent it. If you fail at your end and mats develop, have your dog shaved and start again. Do not subject him to pain because you were careless and now are attached to a certain "look." Hair grows back; trust doesn't.

ALSO SUITED FOR

Family Dog, Nine-to-Five Dog, City Dog, Watchdog.

SARAH WILSON

Bouvier des Flandres

USUAL PLUSES

As adults, they are usually calm in the house, yet ready to play at a moment's notice. One-family dogs, these guys are seldom interested in anyone but you.

When properly bred, raised, and trained, these gentle and patient dogs can be terrific with kids. Don't let their laid-back nature fool you, though—this is an extremely bright dog capable of a high level of training. Naturally protective, they take their job of guardian seriously.

POSSIBLE DRAWBACKS

These are strong-willed dogs. Take the leadership position or be led—there is no middle ground. Can be overprotective; some are shy, some fight with other dogs, and some nip at heels. This is not a dog for casual owners. Be ready to invest time the first few years in making verbal control a habit. It is time well spent.

As with many of these breeds, if allowed to raise themselves with little training or direction, Bouviers can become a behavioral hazard. Properly educated and supervised, this is a calm breed that will watch over every member of your family with equal commitment.

HEIGHT
23½–27½ inches.

WEIGHT
Around 65–100 pounds.

COLOR
Fawn to black, usually gray.

GROOMING
Professional grooming is mandatory—every 8 weeks with weekly brushing in between. That beard! It seems permanently wet, and will get quite smelly if you don't wash it often.

SHEDDING
Minimal.

TRAINING

Professional assistance is mandatory—from puppyhood on. Bouvs do not suffer fools gladly; never let them think you a fool.

EXERCISE

Mandatory, especially for animals younger than two years old.

CHILDREN

Generally good with children they are raised with.

OTHER PETS

Generally good with animals they are raised with.

BITE POTENTIAL

Low to high.

POSSIBLE HEALTH CONCERNS

Hip dysplasia, bloat, and cancer.

SPECIAL COMMENTS

Be prepared for the "Bouvier flop." They don't just lie down, they lift up all four feet at once and plummet earthward. It sounds like a small car hitting the house. This is perfectly normal, if a tad disconcerting at first.

ALSO SUITED FOR

Watchdog, Not for Everyone.

SARAH WILSON

Cairn Terrier

USUAL PLUSES

You remember Toto from *The Wizard of Oz*, right? Mischievous, devoted, naughty, fun-loving, he barked at the flying monkeys and never left Dorothy's side unless something needed chasing? That's a Cairn!

POSSIBLE DRAWBACKS

These are terriers, so some will bark, almost all will dig, most will chase other animals, many will think they know best and, often, they will. These little dogs think big; they will guard their yard and people from all danger. His willingness to assert himself, however, can backfire on the owner if the dog is not trained, socialized, or managed properly.

Cairns are explorers at heart; they love to investigate everywhere and everything. Make sure your fencing is secure, your cabinets are shut, and your household chemicals are safely stored.

HEIGHT
9½–10 inches.

WEIGHT
About 13–14 pounds.

COLOR
Any color except white.

GROOMING
Minimal.

SHEDDING
Minimal. Soft undercoat will shed out twice a year, but regular combing will keep that under control.

TRAINING
Yes, especially "Leave it" and "Come," but don't bank on them. Keep your Cairn on-lead or in a fenced-in area.

EXERCISE
Moderate.

CHILDREN

Calm Cairns are good with calm children.

OTHER PETS

They can enjoy the company of other dog friends, but don't be surprised at their vocal play. It is normal for Cairns to growl ferociously when tussling. Early socialization, neutering, and caution around male-to-male interaction are advised. Acceptance of cats varies from dog to dog. Cairns are best if raised with and taught early to respect feline family members.

BITE POTENTIAL

Low to high, depending on the individual.

POSSIBLE HEALTH CONCERNS

Few—they are a hardy breed. Dental problems are commonplace, so at-home tooth care and veterinary attention twice a year is often necessary.

JILL ARNEL

SPECIAL COMMENTS

Not usually a fawning breed, they are, however, attuned to their owner's mood with an almost eerie accuracy.

Be very careful around moving objects, as many Cairns react fiercely to bicycles, motorcycles, cars, noisy trucks, and the like. If they are not on-lead or behind a fence, they will get hurt.

ALSO SUITED FOR

City Dog, Watchdog.

Chinese Crested

USUAL PLUSES

There are two types of Cresteds: Hairless and Powder Puff. The Hairless actually have a tuft on the top of their head and a fuzzy go-go boot on each leg. The Powder Puffs have a more traditional coat of fine, long fur. Both are charming, utterly devoted little dogs. At first I thought the Hairless were weird-looking, but as I grew fond of one in particular, I began to think her sleek, elegant, and muscular; love can change your mind. These dogs serve as living hot-water bottles and make good little watchdogs.

POSSIBLE DRAWBACKS

While brushing is clearly not necessary for the hairless ones, skin care is. Regular baths, moisturizers, suntan lotions and more are part of day-to-day life.

Socialize well, as they can be shy. Keep them on-lead; they can take off after a squirrel or rabbit in a second. Cresteds need clothing (some folks think of it as a plus). Sweaters in the winter—often more than one outside and a warm one for around the house. In the summer they need a T-shirt until their tan develops a bit. Yes, they can get a sunburn.

Lastly, are you ready for other people's comments? Common ones are "What's wrong with your dog?" or "Did your dog have chemotherapy?" Both are well meaning, but the remarks can become annoying.

HEIGHT

Ideally, 11–13 inches.

WEIGHT

Not specified.

COLOR

Any.

GROOMING

Hairless need regular baths, moisturizers, and sunblock application. They can be prone to blackheads. Powder Puffs need minimal but regular grooming.

SHEDDING

Hairless: None. Powder Puff: Minimal.

TRAINING

Okay, if you want.

EXERCISE

Yes, though active indoor games can suffice in inclement weather.

CHILDREN

Older children with better motor control and intentions are well suited to this breed.

OTHER PETS

Usually fine. Can torment cats if not taught otherwise. Do not pair with much larger dogs, as injury is likely.

BITE POTENTIAL

Low.

POSSIBLE HEALTH CONCERNS

Healthy group, on the whole. The hairless members of this breed suffer from dental problems and early tooth loss. Both can have subluxating patellas, Legg-Calves Perthes disease, and eye problems.

SPECIAL COMMENTS

Long-lived. Expect to enjoy your Crested's company for 13 years or more.

ALSO SUITED FOR

City Dog, Indoor Companion, Watchdog.

Miniature Schnauzer

USUAL PLUSES

Compact, generally long-lived, devoted dogs with a self-confidence and sense of humor their devotees find absolutely charming. Happy "talking" is not uncommon. One of our favorite clients, a salt-and-pepper mini named Sophie, does a happy little yodel when joy grabs ahold of her. These are extremely interactive and expressive animals.

POSSIBLE DRAWBACKS

Can be noisy. Extremely sensitive and people-attached, some of these dogs can be a bit needy. These are terriers, so some are scrappy around other dogs, most will give hearty chase to smaller animals, and a few will be snappish. In general, softer and easier to control than some of the other terriers.

HEIGHT
12–14 inches.

WEIGHT
Under 15 pounds.

COLOR
Black, black and silver, salt and pepper.

GROOMING
Professional grooming required every 6 to 8 weeks to keep your Mini neat and tidy. Furnishings (hair on the legs) are prone to small knots, so weekly combing is in order.

SHEDDING
Minimal to none.

TRAINING
Absolutely—this is a terrier.

EXERCISE
They both enjoy and need it, but because of their size, they have moderate needs.

CHILDREN

Most are good.

OTHER PETS

Normally fine.

BITE POTENTIAL

Low to high.

POSSIBLE HEALTH CONCERNS

Some penchant for bladder and kidney disease. Also allergies, diabetes, pancreatitis, some progressive retinal atrophy.

SPECIAL COMMENTS

Minis can be prone to paw licking and foot chewing. This can be attributed to boredom, stress, habit, allergies, or a combination of the above. Since treatments vary depending on the cause, speak to your vet and your breeder if your dog starts bothering his feet.

ALSO SUITED FOR

City Dog (but watch the barking), Watchdog

LORI McCARTHY

Portuguese Water Dog

USUAL PLUSES

PWDs are versatile, fun-loving, medium-sized dogs who want to be with you doing something—ideally something in the water. These dogs can take center stage in almost any dog activity, including agility, pet therapy, obedience, tracking, water rescue, and more.

POSSIBLE DRAWBACKS

Their standard calls for these dogs to be "very resistant to fatigue," and most fulfill that requirement admirably. Natural retrievers, a PWD feels most comfortable with something in her mouth. Expect mouthing, object stealing, and chewing unless she is supervised, directed, and confined appropriately when young.

We have seen a wide range of temperaments in these dogs, so proceed with care. Shyness plus weirdness run in some lines. Accept only a calm, stable pup from a calm, stable mother.

HEIGHT

17–23 inches.

WEIGHT

35–60 pounds.

COLOR

Black, white, brown, and any combination of brown or black with white.

GROOMING

Professional attention is mandatory every 6 to 8 weeks, with weekly brushing in between.

SHEDDING

None.

TRAINING

Highly trainable, PWDs benefit from the partnership and direction good training develops. Early socialization and puppy kindergarten are recommended if any tendencies toward shyness exist.

EXERCISE

Mandatory. This is a rugged, working breed that wants a job to do. An hour or more of exercise a day is required. Too little, and problems will absolutely develop.

CHILDREN

A stable PWD is a lovely, if active, family dog.

OTHER PETS

Usually fine.

BITE POTENTIAL

Low, in a stable animal.

POSSIBLE HEALTH CONCERNS

Progressive retinal atrophy, hip dysplasia, Addison's disease, follicular dysplasia. The national breed club works hard to track genetic disease. Using a blood test that can be done when a pup is just a few weeks old, they have gotten a good handle on the storage disease that used to plague this breed. This club is to be applauded for their efforts on behalf of the breed they so clearly love.

JUDITH SCHUTZMAN

SPECIAL COMMENTS

Loves to swim, so take him to the water when you can.

ALSO SUITED FOR

Family Dog; High-Input, High-Output Dog; Watchdog.

Soft-Coated Wheaten Terrier

USUAL PLUSES

People get Wheatens because they are playful, friendly, medium-sized, and adorable-looking. Outgoing and active, a Wheaten is no couch potato. Leaping, spinning, romping, cavorting, Wheatens love to do things! They can catch flying disks, race over agility courses, win in flyball (a team retrieving competition over jumps), herd sheep, hike mountains, and even compete in field trials! If you really want to appreciate this dog's mind, work him!

POSSIBLE DRAWBACKS

Busy, active, alert—this dog can be more than you bargained for. A fine choice for calm but active people, this is not a great choice for hyperactive people, as the dog will pick up the energy in the house.

Wheatens are terriers, so some will be diggers, fighters, barkers, and fence stormers. Some will resist training, and males especially may try to assert themselves if they think they can. Independent thinkers, they tend to amuse themselves—a trait that is both a plus and a minus. Neuter early to avoid leg-lifting problems. Housebreak carefully from the start, as some can take a long time.

HEIGHT

17–19 inches

WEIGHT

30–40 pounds.

COLOR

Color of wheat, thus the name. Born dark, Wheatens lighten as they mature.

GROOMING

Professional assistance is mandatory. Bred for profuse, often cottony fur, this is a high-maintenance arrangement if you elect to keep them in full coat. We recommend a shorter trim and thorough brushing at least three times a week. If the dog gets wet, you'll need to groom him, as he mats easily.

SHEDDING

Minimal.

TRAINING

Mandatory. Wheatens are bubbly, distractible, and often free thinkers. They are trainable and bright when they are paying attention. Your job is to get that attention. Wheatens put on some of the best "I'm too pathetic" acts around. If they learn that this gets them out of complying, you are sunk!

EXERCISE

Mandatory. This is an active breed that needs daily romps and walks to be content.

CHILDREN

Normally good, provided they are trained not to mouth or jump, at least most of the time. If allowed to be out of control, they can be overly assertive with children.

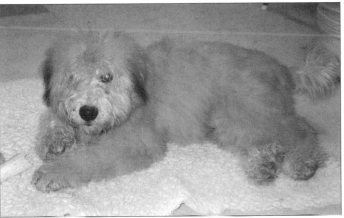
SUZANNAH VALENTINETTI

OTHER PETS

Normally fine, though two males may get into trouble.

BITE POTENTIAL

Moderate.

POSSIBLE HEALTH CONCERNS

Kidney problems affect approximately one-sixth of Wheatens. These problems are not yet well understood. Skin and eye problems are also present. Careful with medication and anesthesia—some Wheatens are sensitive!

SPECIAL COMMENTS

We never recommend pet stores, but be particularly careful about pet-store Wheatens. Some of the Wheatens we've seen have epic housebreaking problems that go far beyond the standard housebreaking difficulties rampant in pet-store pups.

ALSO SUITED FOR

High-Input, High-Output Dog; Watchdog.

Standard Schnauzer

USUAL PLUSES

A medium-sized dog with a giant-sized view of the world. Serious, fearless, alert, high-spirited—this breed never misses a trick. And, for better or worse, they do not forget the things they learn.

Sturdy, ready-for-anything dogs, they compete in agility, obedience, tracking, search-and-rescue, pet-therapy work, and some even herd. If you want a quiet companion who'll lie at your feet and never have a thought in his head, a Standard is *not* for you. If you want an active, bright canine partner, consider a Standard.

POSSIBLE DRAWBACKS

Bred to guard the farm and kill the vermin, these guys can be quick on the draw, so get excellent verbal control or maintain physical control; consider keeping his lead on at the door. Don't expect Standard Schnauzers to fawn on guests. Predatory, so keep on-lead or in a fenced area. If they spot a squirrel, they'll be off.

Convince these determined dogs early that you are a leader worth following and then never relinquish that leadership. Don't use emotion or violence to do this convincing; only consistency and fairness will impress them.

HEIGHT
17½–19½ inches.

WEIGHT
Around 35–45 pounds.

COLOR
Salt and pepper, solid black.

GROOMING
Professional grooming is mandatory.

SHEDDING
Low to none.

TRAINING
Professional assistance is mandatory. These are high-powered, intelligent dogs that need effective training to be their best. Not a do-it-at-home project. Successfully

owning and raising a Golden Retriever does not qualify you as an experienced owner ready for a Standard.

EXERCISE
Mandatory.

CHILDREN
Fine, if raised with them, and supervised and trained.

OTHER PETS
Again, if raised with others, supervised, and trained, Standards are fine, though I would not keep two same-sex animals together.

BITE POTENTIAL
Moderate.

MARILEE SCHAFER

POSSIBLE HEALTH CONCERNS
Generally healthy and hardy. Live a long time (normally 12-plus years). Some hip dysplasia and progressive retinal atrophy (as in so many breeds), but not an overwhelming problem at this time.

SPECIAL COMMENTS
This is not a Nine-to-Five Dog. Standards want and need to be involved in your life.

ALSO SUITED FOR
High-Input, High-Output Dog; Watchdog; Not for Everyone.

West Highland White Terrier

USUAL PLUSES

Besides adorable? Along with the Australian, Cairn, Norfolk, Norwich, and Border Terriers, the Westie rounds out the "not-so-aggressive-for-a-terrier" club. Eager, active, and fun-loving, Westies make nice companion terriers. Westies like people and will usually glad-hand anyone they meet.

POSSIBLE DRAWBACKS

May have flea allergies as well as other skin problems. Can be barky; most will dig. Along with the rest of their clan, they love to chase moving objects. Squirrels can be a lifetime obsession. General feistiness is not uncommon. On-leash or inside a fence only!

HEIGHT

10–11 inches.

WEIGHT

15–19 pounds.

COLOR

White.

GROOMING

Professional care is mandatory if you want your Westie to resemble the pictures in books. A trip to the groomer every 6 to 8 weeks is key. If professionally and regularly groomed, maintenance is minimal. Coat sheds dirt surprisingly well. A thorough, weekly brushing is all that's required.

SHEDDING

Minimal to none.

TRAINING

Yes—it's a terrier.

EXERCISE

See training.

CHILDREN

Okay with older children. Few terriers tolerate toddler mauling with good humor—some may hide, some may snap.

OTHER PETS

Do not put same-sex or same-age dogs together. They love to chase things—how agile is your cat?

BITE POTENTIAL

Moderate, though some poorly bred specimens can be unreliable.

POSSIBLE HEALTH CONCERNS

As with so many all-white dogs, deafness and chronic skin complaints can be a problem. Besides some cases of copper toxicosis and Legg-Calves Perthes disease, Westies are fairly healthy little dogs.

SPECIAL COMMENTS

The West Highland White Terrier Club of America works hard to identify and control genetic disease. Be sure to contact them if you are considering a Westie. You can get their address from the American Kennel Club (listed in "Resources" in the back of this book).

ALSO SUITED FOR

City Dog, Watchdog.

CHRISTINE SWINGLE

Other dogs that are also low-shed breeds:

Maltese

Miniature Poodle

Norfolk Terrier

Norwich Terrier

Standard Poodle

Tibetan Terrier

Toy Poodle

Welsh Terrier

Yorkshire Terrier

The Watchdog

With the exception of some sighthounds that just don't understand the point of barking when someone is at the door, most dogs will give you warning when a stranger approaches. Size doesn't matter in the world of watchdogs. Some of the smallest breeds are the best alarms. A watchdog alerts you to the presence of a problem. A guard dog tries to handle the problem. Be careful of the guard dogs.

JOANNE SILVER

As seductive as having a battle-ready canine determined to protect you and your family sounds, the reality is quite different. As frightening as our world may seem on the TV screen, most of us live fairly peaceful lives. We are not under attack. We do not have people breaking into our homes on a regular basis. What we do have are people we cherish. We have children whose friends stampede through the house daily. A protective dog can make bad decisions about little Joey from next door who comes into your yard unannounced, or friend Mary who runs into the house to use the bathroom. These are the people who need to be kept safe.

Dogs with high bite potential need special training and supervision. Because they are forceful, confident dogs, acquiring one should be a family decision. Every person in your home must direct the dog, the children with the assistance of an adult. If one person does all the work, you may create a dog that listens to and respects only that caretaker. In most homes, we recommend a female of these high-powered breeds.

Chesapeake Bay Retriever

USUAL PLUSES

Loyal and serious, the Chessie is a smart dog that requires smart handling. Unlike the other retrievers, Chessies have a well-developed protective instinct. Bred to hunt with his owner, then guard his gear at the end of the day, this is not a dog that is going to slink away from a fight. Because of this, some people find themselves in over their heads. Early socialization and training brings out the best in this noble dog.

POSSIBLE DRAWBACKS

Earn your dog's respect early and keep it. Respect is earned by consistent, sensible leadership. If you let things slide, don't get angry that the dog does what you've allowed him to do: ignore you. These strong dogs can and will think for themselves. They enter your house sure that they do know best, and it is up to you to convince them otherwise.

Protective and territorial dogs, Chessies should not be let off-lead unless you are 100 percent sure of their socialization and of your control.

Chessies may fight with other dogs. As with all retrievers, they can be chewers early in life, so crate training is necessary.

HEIGHT
21–26 inches.

WEIGHT
55–80 pounds.

COLOR
Various shades of brown.

GROOMING
Minimal.

SHEDDING
Moderate.

TRAINING
Professional assistance is mandatory. This is not a Lab with a wavy coat. Puppy classes and socialization are a must. Do the work yourself; do not send them away.

Chessies bond to you and will work best for you. Chessies are highly trainable—think fun, fair, and firm! You won't go wrong.

EXERCISE

Yes, a lot and daily. They live to swim, so indulge them when you can.

CHILDREN

If you keep a good handle on the dog through training, most Chessies make fine family companions.

OTHER PETS

Usually fine if raised with them, but some Chessies are quite dominant, others predatory. If you have such a dog, introduce other animals into your home with care.

BITE POTENTIAL

Medium to high.

POSSIBLE HEALTH CONCERNS

Hip dysplasia, elbow dysplasia, progressive retinal atrophy, von Willebrand's disease.

SPECIAL COMMENTS

We've heard them called stubborn, but what we see is a dog with low tolerance for inconsistency. If you are willing to stand there and repeat yourself, they are willing to let you. If Chessies see no pilot in the cockpit, they do not panic; they simply don goggles and take the controls. That's not a stubborn dog; that's a good Chessie.

ALSO SUITED FOR

High-Input, High-Output Dog.

Great Pyrenees

USUAL PLUSES

Devoted, calm once mature, quiet, the Great Pyrenees takes his job of watching over your family and your home very seriously. The good news is that he does not need training to do this. He was bred for the work. The bad news is, he does it naturally, which means you will have to get excellent control over him early and maintain it if you hope to be able to direct his behavior.

POSSIBLE DRAWBACKS

Bred to stay with "his" flock and make independent decisions about what needs doing, this is not a dog that hangs on your every word. Unless you socialize him carefully and train him consistently for at least the first three years of his life, you will have a liability on your hands.

Don't expect them to love unfamiliar dogs—this goes double for males. They will chase, and some will attack, strange dogs on their property.

Part of their guard duty is to warn off possible enemies; they do this well and often. Barking is a normal Pyr behavior. Anything new, anyone passing by, any distant sound, any suspicious thing will be barked at. These dogs may frequently circle their domain barking. Originally, it was a way of warning off predators. Remember: Big dogs have big barks.

HEIGHT
25–32 inches.

WEIGHT
90–125 pounds.

COLOR

White with or without biscuit/badger (gray) markings.

GROOMING

Moderate. Weekly brushings will keep things in order.

SHEDDING

Moderate most of the year but because of the sheer bulk we're talking about, a lot. During the twice-a-year shed, immense amounts of hair will be lost. People spin it into yarn. . . .

TRAINING

Professional assistance is mandatory, especially during the first three years. Go to class. Keep going. Go all the way through your dog's adolescence. These huge animals are smart and assertive, so gaining immediate verbal control is absolutely essential.

EXERCISE

Good idea. Once mature, these are fairly sedate dogs. But just because they will lie around all day doesn't mean they should. Don't expect them to fetch; they don't much see a point to this game. A long walk is your best bet.

CHILDREN

Normally wonderful, but their large size can cause some toddler knockdowns. It left untrained and unsocialized, they may not be reliable with your kids' friends or their parents.

OTHER PETS

Fine, especially if raised with them. They will naturally include them in the "my job to watch" group.

CHRISTINE M. PELLICANO

BITE POTENTIAL

Moderate, if properly selected, reared, trained, and managed.

POSSIBLE HEALTH CONCERNS

Surprisingly, hip dysplasia is not as widespread as you might think, but still buy only from OFA parents. Some eyelid problems, but the big killer is bloat. In general, a fairly healthy breed.

SPECIAL COMMENTS

If you think hair is horrendous or barking is bothersome, look at some other breed. The Pyr will give you his heart; he will also give you a lot to clean up. Males should be neutered early.

ALSO SUITED FOR

Nine-to-Five Dog.

Miniature Pinscher

USUAL PLUSES

Bold, alert, active, creative, and athletic—quite a big dog stuffed in that petite package. This dog is always on the go; you will never be bored with a Min Pin! These dogs attach to you with a vengeance and have little use for strangers. A mighty defender that will give his body and soul for you.

POSSIBLE DRAWBACKS

This breed barks. This is not a lapdog any more than Napoleon was a hairstylist. Can be aggressive toward other dogs and hard to housebreak, especially the males. Neuter males early to avoid the leg-lifting problems common to this small dog with a big opinion of himself. Because they are athletic and fearless, containing them can be a challenge.

Socialize, socialize, socialize—the more, the better!

HEIGHT

10–12½ inches.

WEIGHT

9–10 pounds.

COLOR

Red, black and tan, chocolate and tan.

GROOMING

Minimal.

SHEDDING

Minimal to moderate.

TRAINING

Absolutely. Start early and keep going! Socialize, educate, direct, and supervise if you hope to have some control over a Min Pin.

EXERCISE

Absolutely, though many of their needs can be met with indoor romping.

CHILDREN

Not recommended. Few will tolerate rough handling or being hurt. Their size makes them vulnerable, especially as puppies.

OTHER PETS

Okay, if raised with them and taught to be respectful. Avoid putting dogs of the same sex or age together. Although we do not recommend placing larger breeds with toys for safety reasons, we know of several Min Pins that live well with larger dogs because of their "Don't tread on me" attitudes. They are not usually tolerant of strange dogs.

BITE POTENTIAL

Moderate to high.

POSSIBLE HEALTH CONCERNS

Generally a hardy breed. Subluxating patellas, diabetes, some progressive retinal atrophy, and Legg-Calves Perthes disease are in their ranks.

SPECIAL COMMENTS

Can be one-person dogs, can be overprotective and nuisance barkers. Sensitive to the cold; will need a coat for outdoor excursions in cold climates. Generally long-lived—expect 12-plus years.

ALSO SUITED FOR

City Dog, Indoor Companion.

SUZANNAH VALENTINETTI

Norwegian Elkhound

USUAL PLUSES

Bouncy, athletic, bold, friendly, Elkhounds are for people who want an independent, intelligent, protective companion. With proper training and exercise, he is happy most anywhere, so long as he is with you.

POSSIBLE DRAWBACKS

Not simply a pet. These dogs need your time, direction, and commitment to be the best they can be. If you want a casual dog that'll raise himself, do *not* buy an Elkhound.

If you don't teach him to regard you as the leader, you may see overprotectiveness, guarding, disobedience, and aggression toward other dogs.

Barking is not a problem, it is a breed trait. Don't expect a quiet Elkhound. Don't be annoyed by a noisy one. After all, you decided on an Elkhound!

HEIGHT
19½–20½ inches.

WEIGHT
48–55 pounds.

COLOR
Gray.

GROOMING

Moderate. Weekly brushing is important to remove any loose undercoat. This allows more airflow to the skin and will help prevent skin problems.

SHEDDING

Twice a year, and epic.

TRAINING

Professional assistance is mandatory. Here is a strong-willed dog that likes to think for himself. He won't be intimidated into compliance; you must earn his respect and then keep it. Start training and socializing early. Expect to be doing some kind of work with your dog—obedience, agility, tracking—for at least the first few years.

EXERCISE

Mandatory. An active breed. He can control himself if you work at it, but it will take some work.

CHILDREN

Normally good with good kids. Watch for possessiveness, as he may assert himself with less senior members of the "pack."

OTHER PETS

Okay, if raised with them. We would not keep two same-sex or same-age Elkhounds in the same house. Can be hard on cats, especially if the cat is running outside.

BITE POTENTIAL

Moderate.

POSSIBLE HEALTH CONCERNS

Generally a healthy breed. There is some progressive retinal atrophy and some glaucoma. Because of their dense coats, hot spots can occur.

SPECIAL COMMENTS

Watch their weight. Like Beagles and Labs, these guys get chunky easily.

ALSO SUITED FOR

High-Input, High-Output Dog.

LARRY G. LOVIG

Pembroke Welsh Corgi

USUAL PLUSES

Some of the cutest puppies! Smart, trainable, willing, up for anything you are, Pembrokes are wonderful for folks who don't have room for a big dog but don't see themselves as "small dog" people. This is not a small dog in any way besides stature.

POSSIBLE DRAWBACKS

Don't forget, this is a working cattle dog. If not trained and socialized early, their herding heritage can get the best of them. Examples of herding behavior gone awry include nipping at the heels of running children, pursuing fast-moving objects like bicycles, barking, and running in circles. All of this is controllable with training and sensible management.

HEIGHT
10–12 inches.

WEIGHT
25–30 pounds.

COLOR
Black and tan, red, sable, and fawn. Any of these can have white markings.

GROOMING
Little.

SHEDDING
Moderate to a lot.

TRAINING

A lot. So very trainable, it would be a shame to waste the dog's natural ability. So very smart, he'll become creatively mischievous if you don't use that brain for good. No special techniques are needed. You teach, he'll learn.

EXERCISE

Moderate to a lot. Short-legged does not mean low-energy. Keeping him moving and doing will keep him happy.

CHILDREN

Good with good kids if he is socialized with them as a puppy.

OTHER PETS

Generally good.

BITE POTENTIAL

Low to moderate.

POSSIBLE HEALTH CONCERNS

The club publishes lists of OFA and CERF'd dogs, so hip dysplasia and eye problems must be present, if uncommon. Some von Willebrand's disease, cervical disk syndrome, epilepsy, and heart problems have been found, but again, these are not prevalent.

SPECIAL COMMENTS

Long-lived dogs. Their long back needs some protection. Do not encourage these dogs to jump on and off furniture or otherwise put that back at risk. Some males may not get on with other males.

CHRISTINE M. PELLICANO

ALSO SUITED FOR

City Dog.

Pomeranian

USUAL PLUSES

Alert, comical, self-possessed, and busy, Poms have been stealing human hearts for decades. Few creatures are cuter than a Pomeranian puppy. This is a charming breed that enjoys being with people.

POSSIBLE DRAWBACKS

As with most dogs in this section, barking can be a problem if you do not take steps to control it. Teaching the dog what is and is not acceptable will help. Teaching— not yelling, hitting, or hurting. Note here that we said "control," not "eliminate." Poms will bark.

Can be snappy if doted on, carried around, and spoiled. Bold to the point of reckless, these guys may well try to take on dogs many times their size. Keep them on-lead for their own protection.

HEIGHT

6–7 inches.

WEIGHT

3–7 pounds.

COLOR

Any solid color, black and tan or particolor (white with colored patches). In terms of the breed standard, the only no-nos are white markings on a solid or a black and tan.

GROOMING

Thorough brushing twice a week. In general, when brushing is regular, the coat is not prone to matting.

SHEDDING

What do you think? If brushed every couple of days during shedding season, shedding is manageable.

TRAINING

Absolutely. They take readily to training and are too cute for words when they do it. Don't underestimate this breed; they're smart enough to do most anything. Their

Nordic ancestry makes independent thought, and less than immediate response to command, a given.

EXERCISE
Active, but because of their size, outside exercise is not mandatory. It is, however, always appreciated (the more the better), but a Pom can get a pretty good workout racing about the average home.

CHILDREN
Calm children with calm adult dogs. Supervise interactions, as small dogs are easy candidates for accidental injury. Not recommended for small children.

OTHER PETS
Okay if raised with them.

BITE POTENTIAL
Moderate.

POSSIBLE HEALTH CONCERNS
Subluxated patellas, tracheal collapse, dental problems can start early. Progressive retinal atrophy and patent ductus arteriosus.

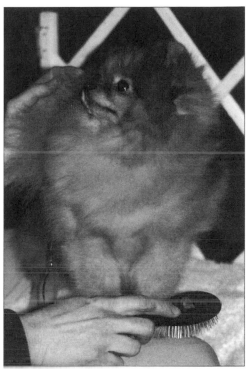

SARAH WILSON

SPECIAL COMMENTS
Neuter males early, no later than 6 months, to help prevent leg-lifting problems. Housebreaking can be a challenge if you don't take it seriously when your Pom is young.

ALSO SUITED FOR
Good Dogs That Are Hard to Find, City Dog, Indoor Companion.

Rhodesian Ridgeback

USUAL PLUSES

Magnificent animals if you like that lean, muscular look. Their usual cowlick down the back, along with their classic good looks, will bring comments wherever you go with this dog.

Devoted and loyal, these dogs are very owner-focused. This is a noble companion for a person who has the time, experience, energy, and willpower to exercise, train, and socialize this fine breed.

Athletic, with excellent endurance and agility, this is a dog that can do many things with ease, be it lure coursing or agility.

POSSIBLE DRAWBACKS

Though they do not lack smarts in any way, some can be prone to reactivity. In other words, they may have big reactions to normal stimulus. These reactions can range from shyness to aggression.

As trainers, we have found some Ridgebacks "hard to access," meaning if you aren't one of the people they love, forget it. Some Ridgebacks take to heart what your mother always said: "Don't talk to strangers."

Serious dogs, they can be aggressive toward other animals and people unless socialized and trained from an early age. Not a casual companion.

HEIGHT
24–27 inches.

WEIGHT
70–85 pounds.

COLOR
Light to dark red-brown.

GROOMING
Minimal.

SHEDDING
Minimal.

TRAINING

Professional assistance is mandatory. This is one large canine muscle with ears. Early socialization and training will help prevent possible shyness, reservation, or aggression problems that can be present in this breed.

EXERCISE

A lot and often. Two long runs or romps a day are the minimum.

CHILDREN

A stable Rhodesian is a lovely dog who will get on well with older, supervised children. An unstable, unsocialized, or misdirected one, though, as with any other large, powerful breed, is not a good choice for anyone.

OTHER PETS

Complicated. Wouldn't put two dogs of the same sex or age together. Usually good with other animals he is raised with. Can be aggressive with animals he does not know.

BITE POTENTIAL

Low to high, depending on the stability of the animal and the commitment of the owner.

POSSIBLE HEALTH CONCERNS

Dermoid sinus, back problems, some deafness.

SPECIAL COMMENTS

Have seen several in the city, where they seem to fare okay if they get the exercise and training they need.

SARAH WILSON

ALSO SUITED FOR

High-Input, High-Output Dog; Not for Everyone.

Dermoid Sinus in Ridgebacks

The dermoid sinus is basically a small tube that extends through the skin of the back toward or into the spine. Some are mild "dead end" types that can be readily fixed with surgery. Others extend into the spinal column itself. Pups with this more advanced form must be euthanized. The problem is normally noted with young pups. Your breeder should have written documentation of their policy (usually replacement or your money back).

Schipperke

USUAL PLUSES

You never have to worry about someone sneaking up on you with this little dynamo nearby. Alert, fearless, and determined; don't mistake this dog for a pushover. He isn't. He would be a guard dog if he had the size to back up his heart. Expect him to protect you with his life.

Trainable, especially with kind consistency and fair firmness. Some superior obedience dogs have been Schipperke. Quick mentally, quick physically, this is a choice for an active, quick-minded human.

Schipp are unusual-looking, sort of a cross between a fox and a miniature hyena. We find them adorable.

POSSIBLE DRAWBACKS

Okay, so this little admiral will warn you of every possible threat, both real and imaginary. Can drive you to distraction if you want to laze around and watch TV all day. These dogs need to *do* things! Now!

Their boldness can lead to bossiness if allowed. As puppies, they are so cute that they are easy to spoil: Don't do it. A Schipp needs excellent, early socialization to balance its natural suspicion of strangers.

HEIGHT
12 inches, plus or minus.

WEIGHT
Up to 18 pounds.

COLOR
Black.

GROOMING
Minimal.

SHEDDING
Average.

TRAINING
Recommended because of their bold nature. They learn quickly and make fun trick dogs. You need to have verbal control because getting your hands on them when

they don't want to be handled is impossible—they are way too quick. Their insatiable curiosity can get them into trouble if you can't control them.

EXERCISE

A lot for his size.

CHILDREN

Good with good, older kids. Normally benevolent to all he considers "his"; some may snap if teased or hurt.

OTHER PETS

Good bet. If raised with them, fine. May not like strange dogs coming onto his property, but few dogs do.

BITE POTENTIAL

Moderate.

POSSIBLE HEALTH CONCERNS

Hardy and healthy. Besides some hypothyroidism, few problems plague the Schipperke.

SPECIAL COMMENTS

Adaptable, fun companion when sensibly socialized and trained.

ALSO SUITED FOR

High-Input, High-Output Dog.

JODI ROBINHOLT

Shetland Sheepdog

USUAL PLUSES

Besides being adorable, bright, and devoted? These dogs spend their time trying to please you. They are playful, charming, and easy to train. Shelties often take top honors at obedience trials. They also excel at agility, pet therapy (taking specially trained dogs to visit the needy), herding, tracking, and flyball.

POSSIBLE DRAWBACKS

High-strung Shelties could test the patience of a saint. These nervous specimens spin nonstop when excited, usually while barking. Shyness is another problem in the breed, so make sure the parents, as well as the puppies, are outgoing and confident. Accept no excuses.

HEIGHT

13–16 inches at the shoulder.

WEIGHT

Normally in the range of 15–20 pounds.

COLOR

Black, sable (tan), and blue merle (gray mottled with black patches). Any of these can have a white ruff, white blaze on the face, white socks (of varying length), and white on the tip of their tail.

GROOMING

Moderate. Weekly brushings paying special attention to the ruff, behind the ears, and the britches should keep your dog looking magnificent.

SHEDDING

Moderate, except during the twice-a-year shedding seasons—then a lot.

TRAINING

Mandatory. Shelties take to training like a duck to water. They yearn to please you. Without guidance, they can become fearful, yappy dogs. This breed wants work and will wilt if treated like a potted plant.

EXERCISE

Small triathlete. Doesn't require the hard miles of the larger active breeds, but still needs daily romps for sanity's sake. Extremely playful, these dogs are not difficult to engage.

CHILDREN

Mostly good with good kids. Small, overly eager human hands can injure small pups. Shy or nervous Shelties can be unreliable. Most will herd the kids if not directed otherwise.

OTHER PETS

Okay.

BITE POTENTIAL

Low to high. Most are loving and tolerant, but some may bite if frightened or hurt.

POSSIBLE HEALTH CONCERNS

Eye, thyroid, skin, hip, knee, and heart problems, von Willebrand's disease, and epilepsy all exist in the population to varying degrees. None of these problems is as prevalent as poor temperament.

SHIRLEY MINATELLI

SPECIAL COMMENTS

At their best, Shelties are dynamic, intelligent, reliable companions. At their worst, they are barky, hide-behind-the-couch, may-bite-the-kids kinds of dogs. Proceed with caution. A good one is well worth finding.

ALSO SUITED FOR

Good Dogs That Are Hard to Find, Family Dog.

Silky Terrier

USUAL PLUSES

Originally a cross between a Yorkie and an Australian Terrier, this breed is as active, bright, entertaining, self-impressed, and generally Napoleonic as that cross implies. If you want a busy, hardy little companion that will make you smile and is game for anything you can think of, consider a Silky. A Silky is an excellent watchdog; he barks at every noise.

POSSIBLE DRAWBACKS

He barks at every noise. Can be feisty with other dogs, leg lifters, and generally strong-minded if not properly selected, socialized, trained, and managed.

Mentally active, excellent problem-solvers, you have to be on your toes to keep up with a Silky. This could be listed under Usual Pluses as well; it just depends on your perspective. It is your job to puppy-proof and keep your mighty mite from harm, as self-protection will not occur to your Silky.

HEIGHT
9–10 inches.

WEIGHT
8–10 pounds.

COLOR
Basically gray and tan.

GROOMING
Yes. A short trim recommended unless you are up for daily coat care.

SHEDDING
Minimal.

TRAINING
Absolutely. Early training and socialization will give you some control over this enthusiastic, mercurial breed.

EXERCISE
A lot is good. Much can be indoor.

CHILDREN

Not the best choice if you have very active, impulsive kids. Though hardy for a toy, these are still small dogs that can be easily hurt.

OTHER PETS

Can be a handful. Can be a cat taunter and a dog boss. Stay away from same-sex canine pairings and larger-dog companions.

BITE POTENTIAL

Moderate to high.

POSSIBLE HEALTH CONCERNS

Subluxating patellas, tracheal collapse, Legg-Calves Perthes disease, diabetes, dental problems, and back problems.

SPECIAL COMMENTS

Neuter early to cut off leg lifting (so to speak) before it starts. Housebreak carefully and crate-train, as getting them clean indoors can be a bit of a challenge if you are lax about it.

ALSO SUITED FOR

Indoor Companion, Low-Shed Breed.

TOM BAUGH

Some of the other good watchdog breeds include:

Airedale

Australian Terrier

Beagle

Bearded Collie

Belgian Sheepdog

Bernese Mountain Dog

Bichon Frise

Boston Terrier

Bouvier des Flandres

Boxer

Cairn Terrier

Cardigan Welsh Corgi

Chihuahua

Collie

Dachshund—(Standard and Miniature)

Doberman Pinscher

German Shepherd Dog

German Shorthaired Pointer

Great Dane

Keeshond

Labrador Retriever

Maltese

Miniature Schnauzer

Norfolk Terrier

Norwich Terrier

Papillon

Petit Basset Griffon Vendeen

Poodle—All Sizes

Portuguese Water Dog

Samoyed

Scottish Terrier

Soft-Coated Wheaten Terrier

Staffordshire Bull Terrier

Standard Schnauzer

Tibetan Terrier

Vizsla

Welsh Terrier

West Highland White Terrier

Yorkshire Terrier

Not for Everyone

SUZANNAH VALENTINETTI

This chapter is written for people who are dog lovers but not necessarily dog experts. Maybe you have never had a dog, maybe you had one growing up, maybe you've had a happy, easy Golden Retriever that never gave you much trouble. If any of these describes you, then you are a beginner dog owner.

The dogs in this section are not "bad" dogs, they just don't usually fit the bill as casual companions for a loving but relatively inexperienced owner. Each breed here is cherished by thousands of devoted fans. Every breed listed can be a happy, stable, reliable companion in a variety of homes. But every breed included has come through our doors a few too many times for us to say they are easy to handle.

A breed is placed in these ranks for many reasons: Maybe they tend to have a challenging temperament or are prone to aggression, maybe they have rampant health problems or popularity has, temporarily, ravaged the breed; frequently, there is a combination of these factors.

We admit up front that our experience is largely based in the Northeast. There can be big regional differences in breeds. To counter this, we did some Internet polling of other professionals to confirm our experience. Now, with over 300 combined years of professional dog training and care behind us, we are confident that these recommendations are sound.

We apologize in advance to all the folks out there who love these dogs dearly. We have faith that you will agree that your breed, as a whole, is not well suited for an inexperienced, casual home.

I'd Never Own a . . .

When we asked other pet professionals (trainers, groomers, vet techs, boarding kennel operators, and pet sitters) what their least favorite breeds were, their top ten responses were as follows:

➤ Chow Chow (95 percent of our respondents listed Chows for temperament reasons)

➤ American Cocker Spaniel (all defended some Cockers as nice, but others were not)

➤ Dalmatian

➤ Lhasa Apso

➤ Old English Sheepdog

➤ Shar Pei (health and temperament reasons)

➤ Akita

➤ Bulldog (health reasons)

➤ Rottweiler

➤ Pit Bull

Also-rans were untrained German Shepherd Dogs, small Poodles, Chesapeake Bay Retrievers, Dobermans, Westies, Scotties, Irish Setters, Saint Bernards, any wolf hybrid, Collies (health reasons), and Yorkies.

Remember, folks: We don't make the news, we just report it.

CHRISTINE M. PELLICANO

Akita

Akitas suffered a population explosion in the 1980s from which ethical breeders are still recovering. While there are sweet-tempered, healthy Akitas, the breed can be more than the average dog owner is ready to take on. Akitas are often powerful, aloof animals that take their own counsel on almost everything. Although many live successfully in the city, do not expect them to be able to play in the dog run without problems. While they will not always start the fight, they will not let small matters (like a bump from another dog) slide. If socialization and training are not taken seriously, this assertiveness may likely be applied to the humans in their lives. Combine this powerful, self-assured temperament with profuse shedding and some major, widespread health problems and the result is a difficult-to-manage pet in inexperienced hands.

American Pit Bull Terrier

Stunningly beautiful, if you like that cut, muscular, Mr. Universe look. Athletic to the max, these powerful animals are normally—and historically—reliable with people. However, they are also powerful animals, many with highly developed predatory instincts. Though responsible breeders have done a lot to temper the breed's temper, they have to fight against the unethical who breed for heightened aggression.

Pits suffer from terrible public relations, which means your pitbull will be held to a higher standard of behavior than your neighbor's, possibly less sane, Golden Retriever. Impulsive, strong-willed, and focused like a laser when stimulated, this breed can do extraordinary things—like leap over six-foot fences, take doors off hinges, and otherwise make every effort to attain their goal. Talk to experts, then think long and hard before introducing this breed into your life. If you are not ready to commit to responsible ownership, careful socialization, and ongoing training, then do yourself, and this wonderful breed, a favor: Select another dog.

Australian Shepherd

Though touted by some as an ideal family dog, we disagree. Chronic barking, shyness, hyperactivity, aggression toward other animals and people, car chasing, and more are all too common in novice pet homes.

This breed has a wide range of temperaments from happy-goofy to hard worker, from intensely shy to dangerously unstable. People tend to believe these dogs are "kind of like a Collie," but this is not so. The standard calls for "intelligent working dogs of

American Staffordshire Terriers

Years ago American Pit Bull Terriers and American Staffordshire Terriers were one and the same, but that hasn't been true for decades. Breeders of American Staffordshire Terriers are always working hard to produce ever more stable, reliable dogs that make wonderful, if powerful, companions. Almost every American Staff ad you see lists temperament as a top priority. American Staffordshire Terriers should not be confused with generic pitbull-type dogs.

strong herding and guarding instinct," and it isn't kidding. In experienced hands these are ultimate competitors, and that's where they belong—in experienced hands.

TONI KAY

Basenji

Known as an independent, playful breed, the Basenji is unlike any other dog we know. They are plenty bright, they just are not all that interested in pleasing you. Charming when they feel like it, elusive when they don't, this dog is unique in its outlook.

Basenjis are quite able to take care of themselves, thank you very much. If you enjoy a beautiful animal that lives alongside you with devotion and joy, then a Basenji is a good choice. If you want a dog that hangs on your every word and accepts all manner of human behavior, you may find this dog frustrating.

Booked as barkless, do not mistake this for "noiseless." They yodel, chortle, and scream—and we do mean scream—when thwarted. Naturally clean, these dogs are normally easy to housebreak but a challenge to train. They don't take well to being directed by others. Convince them that working is their idea, and you have a chance. Use old-fashioned, yank-and-pat methods and you won't get far.

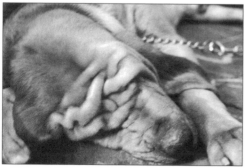

SARAH WILSON

Bloodhound

Much to our surprise, we note that Bloodhounds are rising through the ranks in the AKC registrations. Starting in 67th position in 1993, they came in at 55th in 1997. Perhaps the heir apparent to the wrinkled crown left open by the Chinese Shar Pei (22nd in 1993 to 32nd in 1997), the Bloody is not an easy indoor dog. All those wrinkles, as charming as they are, guarantee a slobber production unimaginable to the average person. If your Bloody is watching you eat and manufacturing drool accordingly, a single shake of his magnificent head can plaster drool on the ceiling, whip it into your cereal bowl, and fling it across your forehead. When you stand up to grab a towel, be careful not to slip in the pool by his feet. This is a big dog with a distinctly focused, tough, hound outlook. If you think the puppy is cute, buy a picture, not a dog. A better tracking animal you will not find, but unless you are pursuing escaped felons, consider another breed.

Border Collie

CHRISTINE M. PELLICANO

5-4-3-2-1, Lift off! These canine whiz kids need things to do—daily. Border Collies are incredible agility dogs, Frisbee catchers, obedience competitors, and herding dogs, but as partially ignored pets expected to curl up at your feet at the end of a long day spent alone, they are miserable.

Even a calm BC is not an easy dog. Think of them as sexy little sports cars: responsive, fast, sleek, but as family vehicles, a nightmare waiting to happen. Shyness, sound-sensitivity, aggression in all forms, chewing, barking, digging, chasing, nipping, and just about anything else you can imagine are all run-of-the-mill behaviors for an undertrained, underutilized BC.

Bulldog

CHRISTINE M. PELLICANO

Since they are possibly the cutest puppies imaginable, who isn't going to fall for these round-headed, big-bodied, snorting little munchkins? Normally laid-back, comical dogs, it is their health challenges, not their temperament, that lands them in this category.

For a dog that is the poster child for big, tough, macho guys, this is one troubled breed. Ranking number two behind the Shar Pei in breeds "Most Likely to Drain Your Wallet at the Veterinarian," the Bulldog is for people with deep pockets. Possible health problems in Bulldogs: The *Control of Canine Genetic Disease* by George A. Padgett, D.V.M., lists 73. Leave the Bulldog to the folks who know their health needs and genetic problems and can handle both.

Chinese Shar Pei

LEWIS HIZER

Unusual-looking and quite a conversation piece, nice Shar Pei adore their owners. When people ask us about this breed we tell them: "A thousand dollars to buy one, a thousand dollars a year to maintain them." Shar Pei have more than their fair share of health problems, from rampant skin disease to practically universal eye surgery(-ies) on puppies. Be sure to choose a vet you like; you'll probably be seeing a lot of her.

Sadly, aggression is all too common in improperly bred, selected, and reared Shar Pei. This unusual breed should be cherished and maintained, but leave that to the people who have the time, the expertise, and the financial status to do so properly. Ranked 22nd in 1993, they are down to 32nd in 1997. This is excellent news. We are sure that devotees of this unusual breed are breathing a collective sigh of relief.

SARAH WILSON

Chow Chow

Chows are serious dogs that form strong attachments to their owners. They often have little interest in, and little tolerance for, strangers. Pet professionals who responded to our Internet poll cited Chows among their least favorite dogs to deal with. Aggression was their complaint. A Chow may be wagging his tail one minute and attached to your forearm the next, with no visible warning in between.

As self-possessed, no-nonsense dogs, Chows require careful consideration, research, selection, training, and management to be their best. Talk at length to Chow Rescue about this breed's needs, sign up for puppy kindergarten before you get your new pet, then go, go, go! Do daily handling with your Chow puppy and, once your vet gives the go-ahead, take your pup with you everywhere.

The good news is that Chows are plummeting in popularity, dropping from 15th in 1993 to 35th in 1997. This should mean that fewer uninformed, profit-motivated people are producing Chows. No doubt with dedicated breeders at the helm, we will see fewer of the difficult dogs and more of the stable ones.

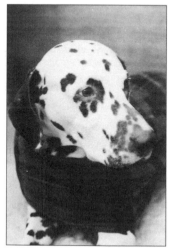
SARAH WILSON

Dalmatian

Dalmatians are photogenic dogs. They appear, in all their considerable glory, in print ads, in movies, and on TV. While they are indeed startlingly handsome, they are also extremely active, shed profusely, and more than a few have aggressive tendencies. Simply put, this is not an easy dog. They need heaping helpings of exercise. A couple of walks a day and free time alone in the backyard will earn you a frustrated Dal. Most of these dogs, especially young ones, need hard running with other dogs, vigorous games of fetch, or long, long brisk walks every day to be content. Dals can have aggressive/protective tendencies, which are both hard for beginners to predict and even harder for them to control. In addition, Dals have some endemic genetic problems, including deafness, urinary-tract problems, and problems digesting certain protein. Only the most knowledgeable breeders with years of study and experience behind them should breed these dogs, and only the educated, experienced, and committed should own them. The right Dal in the right hands is a great dog, but both those dogs and those hands are difficult to come by.

Irish Setter

SARAH WILSON

Standing nobly, their mahogany coats glowing in the sun, Irish Setters are too gorgeous for words. For all their good looks, this breed is not a perfect average pet. Exercise, exercise, exercise is the first order of the day. Irish Setters are born to run and run they will: in circles in your kitchen, or full-out in your fenced-in yard—your choice.

On top of a couple of hours of hard romping a day, young Irish need calm, daily training to develop some much-needed self-control. Of the "Leap first, look later" mind-set, Irish Setters can get into all kinds of mischief when young. They are so gleefully impulsive you may want to just pack up your breakables for the first couple of years!

This is a breed that fought its way back to sanity after a massive population boom in the 1970s. We salute the devoted breeders responsible for their excellent efforts. While these dogs may have left their reputations as dumb redheads behind, they are not a good choice for hectic households, emotional, impatient, or house-proud people, or people with small children. They need a calm yet active household that is fully committed to giving this dog what he needs for the first few years.

Jack Russell Terrier

GWEN BARBA

Made popular in the early 1990s through widely viewed TV shows, this comical and complicated breed rose in numbers. JRTs are bright, athletic, quick terriers. The problem is that they are bright, athletic, quick terriers. Expect to come home and find them atop a bookshelf, having leaped from couch to sideboard to shelves in order to get there. This, however, is not the real problem. The most significant problem facing JRTs comes under the heading of aggression. This is a primitive terrier breed that often responds to stimulation of many kinds with aggression. Frustration can also result in teeth.

Are there stable, sweet JRTs out there? Yup. In our 45 years of combined work, we know of one that never, ever bit. Granted, we see the problem children, but still, no matter what the presenting problem was, aggression was always a subtext. The new AKC standard calls for no aggression of any kind. This is an admirable goal, but at the time of this writing, it has not yet been achieved. Until that day, JRTs need to be kept by people who appreciate their impulsive, feisty terrier nature and will manage them accordingly.

SARAH WILSON

Lhasa Apso

Few people realize that Lhasas were developed as a guard breed in Tibet. Don't let their size or charming looks fool you—these are serious, intelligent dogs that need calm, consistent leadership or they will quietly take over your home. We have met many that had little tolerance for following orders, and they refuse to get off the furniture, drop a coveted piece of garbage, or lie down on command. Unless you start early and work with them consistently, grooming can be a challenge for many pet owners. For small dogs, they bite big!

Caring breeders have made headway in moderating their breed's aggressive tendencies, but it is not yet a breed we can recommend as a casual or family companion.

SARAH WILSON

Old English Sheepdog

This is another breed thrust into popularity by Disney in the 1960s on which popularity took its inevitable toll. At their best, these are happy-go-lucky dogs that love life and their families in equal measure. They are rompers and lickers and a general joy to be around. But there are too many that are still recovering from the effects of overbreeding. Responsible breeders are battling horrible hip problems and some unreliable, snappish temperaments. Add to that a high-maintenance coat and you have a breed that requires expertise to purchase, raise, and maintain. Fortunately, pet buyers are getting wise to this large commitment. OEDs are down from 51st in 1993 to 60th in 1997.

Rottweiler

Rocketing to the top of the popularity charts in the late 1980s, rampant breeding created too many black-and-tan nightmares. Yes, we know, there are thousands of sweet Rotties running around, but that does not mean they are all nice or that you will get a nice one or be able to raise it to be a nice dog.

When I asked Suzanne Kinder, a long-time Rotty owner and professional trainer, what she thought was the biggest mistake novices make with this breed, she replied without hesitation: "Wanting one." They are way too much dog for most homes. This is an intelligent, powerful animal that frequently needs daily training and direction to stay civilized. Most Rottweilers like to be in charge and are more than happy to assume control if given half a chance.

SARAH WILSON

Although this breed still holds the second spot on the AKC's registration statistics, its numbers have dropped considerably. In 1993 they held second place with a staggering 104,160 dogs registered. Last year, 1997, there were 75,489. This is promising news for this fine, but high-maintenance, breed.

Saint Bernard

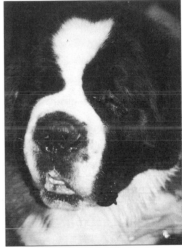
SARAH WILSON

In the 1970s this noble breed was also dealt a media-related mortal wound. Just as the serious Saint people were recovering from that round of irresponsible breeding, along came the 1990s *Beethoven* movies to start the trend all over again. Size alone makes a Saint difficult to manage for all but experienced dog folks. Add to its size some prevalent health concerns, like poor hips and all-too-common temperament problems, and you have an animal that should be cherished by those who know and love it well. A good Saint is, well, a saint: calm, sweet, and easygoing. A bad Saint, or a poorly reared Saint, is a nightmare, a liability, and a heartbreak.

Weimaraner

LEWIS HIZER

The Weims we've met need such tremendous amounts of exercise that few people can accommodate their needs. If not exercised adequately, expect behavior problems. When bored, this is a breed that can chew. And chew. And chew. If confined too much, all kinds of unwanted behaviors can develop, such as hyperactivity, repetitive behaviors (like pacing or circling), barking, and more. These dogs can be quite strong-willed and quite tough. If you have the time for two or more hours of hard running a day for the first three years, the temperament to direct this bright dog firmly, and a lifestyle where the dog would not be alone every day, then by all means consider this stunning breed.

Other breeds that can fall into this category are:

Airedale	German Shepherd Dog
Alaskan Malamute	Rhodesian Ridgeback
Belgian Sheepdog	Siberian Husky
Bouvier des Flandres	Staffordshire Bull Terrier
Bullmastiff	Standard Schnauzer

Resources

Books

BEFORE YOU GET YOUR DOG

The Irrepressible Toy Dog
Darlene Arden
Howell Book House/A Simon & Schuster Macmillan
Company, 1633 Broadway, New York, New York
10019. 1998
A book written by a toy lover for toy lovers. If you are
thinking about getting a toy dog, this is the book you
need to have. Covers just about everything!

Control of Canine Genetic Diseases
George A. Padgett, D.V.M.
Howell Book House/A Simon & Schuster Macmillan
Company, 1633 Broadway, New York, New York 10019. 1998
A comprehensive and sensible look at genetic diseases in dogs. May well contain more than the av-
erage owner wants to know, but the listings of breeds and their attendant genetic problems are well
worth looking at prior to acquiring a companion.

THOMAS WHATLEY

The Roger Caras Dog Book: A Complete Guide to Every AKC Breed
Roger Caras
Dorset House Publishing Company, 353 West 12 Street, New York, New York 10014. 1992
Everything Roger writes—and he writes a lot—is easy to read and interesting. You'll get good in-
formation from his books.

Your Purebred Puppy: A Buyer's Guide
Michele Lowell
Henry Holt and Company, Inc., 115 West 18th Street, New York, New York 10011. 1990
An oldie but a goodie. Sensible, straightforward, informative—we recommend it.

SELECTING YOUR DOG

Good Owners, Great Dogs
Brian Kilcommons and Sarah Wilson
Warner Books, 1271 Avenue of the Americas, New York, New York 10020. 1992
We are pleased to say that a couple hundred thousand of you like this book. We are told that it is

PETER HERNANDEZ

packed with sensible information, a fun read, well designed with great pictures—that's what we were trying for. Has a good section on how to puppy-test a puppy.

Mutts: America's Dogs
Brian Kilcommons and Michael Capuzzo
Warner Books, 1271 Avenue of the Americas,
New York, New York 10020. 1996
Good information on how to select a puppy or adult dog from a shelter. Mutts and purebreds get tested no differently.

The Puppy Report
Larry Shook
Lyons & Burford/The Lyons Press, 31 West 21 Street,
New York, New York 10010. 1992
This book will scare you straight! A true-to-life, carefully researched book about the puppy industry, genetics, and responsibility. Well worth a thoughtful read before you set out puppy hunting.

Understanding Puppy Testing
Suzanne Clothier
Flying Dog Press, P.O. Box 290, Stanton, New Jersey 08885. 1-800-7FLY-DOG.
E-mail: clothier@eclipse.net
Internet: www.flyingdogpress.com
Ms. Clothier's booklets are easy to read, sensible, and short. You won't go wrong ordering any of her wide selection.

AFTER YOU GET YOUR PUPPY

The Canine Good Citizen: Every Dog Can Be One
Jack Volhard and Wendy Volhard
Howell Book House/A Simon & Schuster Macmillan Company,
1633 Broadway, New York, New York 10019. 1994
Nice, sensible, comprehensive book that can help owners understand and live in harmony with their dog.

Childproofing Your Dog
Brian Kilcommons and Sarah Wilson
Warner Books, 1271 Avenue of the Americas, New York, New York 10020. 1994
If you have children in your life, you need to read this small but information-packed book. Prevent problems before they arise!

Dog Owner's Home Veterinary Handbook
Delbert G. Carlson, D.V.M., and James M. Griffin, M.D.
Howell Book House/A Simon & Schuster Macmillan Company,
1633 Broadway, New York, New York 10019. Revised edition 1992

Well written, well indexed, and well thought out, this remains the book we pull off the shelves in our home when we have questions. An excellent resource.

Tails from the Barkside
Brian Kilcommons and Sarah Wilson
Warner Books, 1271 Avenue of the Americas, New York, New York 10020. 1997
Fun-filled stories guaranteed to make dog lovers giggle. If you look at them as instructional guides on what not to do, it can even help with your new dog. Otherwise, just read for the fun of it.

UCDavis Book of Dogs: A Complete Medical Reference Guide for Dogs and Puppies
Faculty and staff, School of Veterinary Medicine, University of California at Davis
Edited by Mordecai Siegal; consulting editor, Jeffery E. Barlough
HarperCollins Publishers, 10 East 53 Street, New York, New York 10022. 1995
A well-written and comprehensive guide to dog care and management. If you are a budding dog fanatic, you'll find this a worthy addition to your library.

Magazines

The AKC Gazette: The Official Journal
for the Sport of Purebred Dogs
5580 Centerview Drive,
Raleigh, North Carolina 27606-3390
Phone: 919-233-9767
Fax: 919-233-3627
Internet: www.akc.org

Dog Fancy
P.O. Box 53264, Boulder, Colorado 80322-3264
Phone: 303-786-7306
Internet: www.dogfancy.com

Dog World
29 North Wacker Drive, Chicago, Illinois 60606
Phone: 312-609-4340
Fax: 312-236-2413
E-mail: dogworld3@aol.com
Internet: www.dogworldmag.com

Internet Sites

There are a lot of dog-related Internet sites. Excellent ones spring up daily, others fall away. Because of this constant

TONI KAT

flux, we are hesitant to recommend any. Nevertheless, here are a few useful ones. Just remember, they are just the tip of the iceberg.

www.canismajor.com
www.cyberpet.com
www.doglogic.com
www.k9web.com

Large Registries

The American Kennel Club
  5580 Centerview Drive, Raleigh, North Carolina 27606-3390
  Customer Service: 919-233-9767
  Write to them for a free AKC Dog Buyers' Education Packet. The AKC can supply you with contact information for national and local breed clubs, rescue groups, and a lot of other good information.

United Kennel Club
  100 East Kilgore Road, Kalamazoo, Michigan 49002-5584
  Phone: 616-343-9020
  This group registers all the breeds the AKC does and a few more.

Books and Videos

Direct Book Service
Dog and Cat Book Catalog
  P.O. Box 2778, Wenatchee, Washington 98807-2778
  Phone: 800-776-2665
  E-mail: dgctbook@cascade.net
  Internet: www.dogandcatbooks.com
  Our favorite source. I defy any dog lover to thumb through this catalog and not buy something.

STACEY SAMELA

Index

Activity, 41
   unwanted, 53
Adoption Option (Rubenstein and Kalina), 34
Adult dogs, selection of, 33–34
Afghans, 45–46
Aggression, 43–45, 47
   dog-to-dog, 44
   territorial, 44–45
Airedales, 146, 232, 242
   as low-shed breed, 188–89
Akbashes, 42–43
AKC Gazette: The Official Journal for the Sport of Purebred Dogs, The, 245
Akitas, 25, 27
   as not-for-everyone dogs, 234
Alaskan Malamutes:
   as high-input, high-output dogs, 124–25
   as sled dogs, 2, 9, 50–51, 124–25, 242
American Cocker Spaniels, 23–25, 39–40, 76, 120, 168, 234
   as hard-to-find dogs, 64–65
American Kennel Club, The (AKC), 17, 22, 27, 47, 74, 78, 119, 144, 209, 236, 241, 246
American Pit Bull Terriers, 234–35
American Staffordshire Terriers, *see* Staffordshire Bull Terriers
Arden, Darlene, 243
Athletes, 50
Australian Shepherds:
   as herding dogs, 12, 23–24, 53–54, 58, 146, 235–36
   as not-for-everyone dogs, 235–36
Australian Terriers, 168, 208, 230, 232
   as low-shed breed, 190–91

Babies, 11–13
   puppies with, 11–12
   see also Children

Bad attitudes, 52
Bad behaviors, 3
Barking, 48, 54
Barlough, Jeffery E., 245
Basenjis, 236
Basset Hounds:
   as city dogs, 148–49
   as scent hounds, 43–45, 82, 148–49
Beagles:
   as hard-to-find dogs, 66–67
   Pocket Beagles, 67
   as scent hounds, 23–25, 43–45, 66–67, 219, 232
Bearded Collies, 122, 232
   as high-input, high-output dogs, 126–27
Beethoven, 241
Belgian Malinois, 128
Belgian Sheepdog Club, 129
Belgian Sheepdogs, 24, 232, 242
   as high-input, high-output dogs, 128–29
Belgian Tervurens, 24, 128
Bernese Mountain Dogs:
   as draft/rescue dogs, 24, 49–50, 102–5, 232
   as family dogs, 103–5
Bichon Frises, 23, 102, 122, 168, 232
   as low-shed breed, 192–93
Bite potential, 61
Bloat, 23
Bloodhounds:
   as not-for-everyone dogs, 236
   as scent hounds, 43–45, 236
Books, 15–16, 243–46
Border Collies:
   as herding dogs, 5, 53–54, 146, 237
   as not-for-everyone dogs, 237
Border Terriers, 208
Borzois:
   as nine-to-five dogs, 84–85
   as sighthounds, 45–46, 84–85

Boston Terriers, 76, 186, 232
   as city dogs, 150–51
Bouvier des Flandres, 9, 12, 24, 232, 242
   as low-shed breed, 194–95
Boxers:
   as high-input, high-output dogs, 130–31
   as property guards, 23, 46–49, 82, 130–31, 232
Breeds, breeding, and breeders, 5, 22, 57–61
   for field or show, 38
   giant, 13–14
   least favorite, 234
   popularity of, 63
   resources on, 15–17
   selection of, 26–28
   small, 14
   visits to, 30–32
Brittany Spaniels:
   as high-input, high-output dogs, 132–33
   as pointers, 27, 40–41, 122, 132–33
Bulldogs, 24–25
   as not-for-everyone dogs, 234, 237
   French Bulldogs, 26, 88–89, 168
Bullmastiffs, 24, 102, 122, 242
   as city dogs, 152–53

Cairn Terriers, 25, 35–37, 168, 208, 232
   as low-shed breed, 196–97
Cancer, 23
Canine Eye Registry Foundation (CERF), 23, 25
Canine Good Citizen: Every Dog Can Be One,
   The (Volhard and Volhard), 244
Capuzzo, Michael, 34, 244
Caras, Roger, 243
Cardigan Welsh Corgis, 232
   as city dogs, 154–55
Cardiomyopathy, 23
Carlson, Delbert G., 244–45
Cataracts, 23
Cavalier King Charles Spaniels, 23, 77, 102, 168
   as family dogs, 106–7
Chasing behaviors, 53
Chesapeake Bay Retrievers, 23, 37–39, 146, 224
   as watchdogs, 212–13
Chihuahuas, 26, 82, 168, 232
   as indoor companions, 172–73

Childproofing Your Dog (Kilcommons and
   Wilson), 244
Children, 60, 170
   dogs for, 4, 6
   see also Babies
Chinese Cresteds, 25, 102, 168
   as low-shed breeds, 198–99
Chinese Shar Peis:
   as non-sporting/rare breed, 54, 234,
      236–38
   as not-for-everyone dogs, 234, 236–38
Chow Chows:
   as non-sporting/rare breed, 54, 234, 238
   as not-for-everyone dogs, 234, 238
City dogs, 147–68
   Basset Hounds, 148–49
   Boston Terriers, 150–51
   Bullmastiffs, 152–53
   Cardigan Welsh Corgis, 154–55
   Norfolk Terriers, 158–59
   Norwich Terriers, 158–59
   Scottish Terriers, 160–61
   Shiba Inus, 162–63
   Standard Dachshunds, 156–57
   Tibetan Terriers, 164–65
   Welsh Terriers, 166–67
Clothier, Suzanne, 32, 244
Cocker Spaniels, see American Cocker Spaniels;
   English Cocker Spaniels
Collie eye anomaly (CEA), 23–24
Collies:
   Bearded Collies, 122, 126–27, 232
   Border Collies, 5, 53–54, 146, 237
   as family dogs, 108–9
   as herding dogs, 5, 23–25, 53–54, 82, 108–9,
      122, 126–27, 146
   rough variety of, 108–9
   smooth variety of, 108–9
Colors, 58–59
Comfort seeking, 46
Commitment, 19
Common sense, 10
Compliant behavior, 39
Control of Canine Genetic Disease (Padgett), 237,
   243

Corgis:
    Cardigan Welsh Corgis, 154–55, 232
    Pembroke Welsh Corgis, 122, 154, 220–21
Crate-training, 149

Dachshunds, 82
    Longhaired Dachshunds, 156, 181
    Miniature Dachshunds, 156, 168, 180–81, 232
    Smooth Dachshunds, 156
    Standard Dachshunds, 156–57, 232
    Wirehaired Dachshunds, 156
Dalmatians:
    as non-sporting/rare breed, 1, 54, 103, 234,
      238–39
    as not-for-everyone dogs, 234, 238–39
Deafness, 44–45
    nasal-related, 44
    running-related, 45
Dehydration, 14
Delta Society, 99
Dermoid sinus, 225
Diggers, 50
Doberman Pinschers:
    as hard-to-find dogs, 68–69
    as property guards, 23, 26–27, 46–49, 68–69,
      146, 232, 234
Dog and Cat Book Catalog, 246
Dog Fancy, 215
Dog Owner's Home Veterinary Handbook
    (Carlson and Griffin), 244–45
Dogs:
    best time to get one, 10–12
    demands of, 6–10
    driving them crazy, 7
    in needing to be needed, 9
    older, 12–13
    with other pets, 60–61
    reasons for wanting them, 4–6
    responsibilities in caring for, 5
    selection of, 12–14, 30–34, 243–44
    younger, 12
    see also puppies
Dog-to-dog aggression, 44
Dog World, 20, 245
Draft/rescue dogs, 49–50

Bernese Mountain Dogs, 24, 49–50, 102–5,
    232
Newfoundlands, 14, 24, 49–50, 114–15, 146
Saint Bernards, 9, 25, 49–50, 234, 241
see also Sled dogs

Education, 7–8
Elbow dysplasia (ED), 24
Emotion, 6–7
Endurance, 40
Energy, 6
English Cocker Spaniel Club of America, 87
English Cocker Spaniels, 39–40, 76, 122, 168
    as nine-to-five dogs, 86–87
English Setters, 41
    as family dogs, 110–11
English Springer Spaniels, 24–25, 28, 39–40, 146
    as hard-to-find dogs, 70–71
Entropion, 24
Epilepsy, 24
Excavating behavior, 36
Exercise, 60

Family dogs, 103–22
    Bernese Mountain Dogs, 103–5
    Cavalier King Charles Spaniels, 106–7
    Collies, 108–9
    English Setters, 110–11
    Keeshonds, 112–13
    Newfoundlands, 114–15
    Samoyeds, 116–17
    Standard Poodles, 103, 118–19
    Welsh Springer Spaniels, 120–21
Fearlessness, 36
Females, 12
Field, breeding for, 38
Flat-Coated Retrievers, 23, 122
    as high-input, high-output dogs, 134–35
Flock guards, 42–43
    Akbashes, 42–43
    Great Pyrenees, 14, 28–29, 42–43, 102, 214–15
    Komondors, 42–43
    Kuvases, 42–43
    see also Property guards; Watchdogs
Foundation for Pet Provided Therapy, 99

Freeman, Muriel, 28
French Bulldogs, 26, 168
    as nine-to-five dogs, 88–89
Friendliness, 38–39

Garbage eating, 44
Genetic disease, 19–26
    avoidance of, 22
    crib notes on, 22–26
Gentleness, 49
German Shepherd Dogs:
    as hard-to-find dogs, 72–73
    as herding dogs, 13, 23–25, 28, 53–54, 58,
       72–73, 232, 234, 242
    as not-for-everyone dogs, 234, 242
German Shorthaired Pointers, 9, 40–41, 232
    as high-input, high-output dogs, 136–37
Giant breeds, 13–14
Giant Schnauzers, 46–49
Golden Retrievers, 19, 23–25, 37–39, 58, 122,
    235
    as hard-to-find dogs, 73–74
Good Owners, Great Dogs (Kilcommons and
    Wilson), 32, 243–44
Gordon Setters, 41
Great Danes:
    as hard-to-find dogs, 76–77
    as property guards, 13–14, 23, 26–28, 46–49,
       76–77, 102, 232
Great Pyrenees:
    as flock guards, 14, 28–29, 42–43, 102, 214–15
    as watchdogs, 214–15
Gregariousness, 39
Greyhounds:
    Italian Greyhounds, 26, 168, 174–75
    as nine-to-five dogs, 90–91
    as sighthounds, 26, 45–46, 90–91, 122, 168,
       174–75
Griffin, James M., 244–45
Groomers and grooming, 16–18, 59

Hard-to-find dogs, 63–82
    American Cocker Spaniels, 64–65
    Beagles, 66–67
    Doberman Pinschers, 68–69
    English Springer Spaniels, 70–71

German Shepherd Dogs, 72–73
Golden Retrievers, 73–74
Great Danes, 76–77
Labrador Retrievers, 78–79
Miniature Poodles, 80–81
Toy Poodles, 80–81
Health:
    concerns about, 61
    tests for, 20–21, 24, 26, 30
    see also specific disorders
Height standards, 58
Herding dogs, 53–54
    Australian Shepherds, 12, 23–24, 53–54, 58,
       146, 235–36
    Border Collies, 5, 53–54, 146, 236
    Collies, 5, 23–25, 53–54, 82, 108–9, 122,
       126–27, 146, 232, 234–36
    German Shepherd Dogs, 13, 23–25, 28,
       53–54, 58, 72–73, 232, 234, 242
    Shetland Sheepdogs, 24–26, 47, 53–54, 82,
       122, 228–29
High-input, high-output dogs, 123–46
    Alaskan Malamutes, 124–25
    Bearded Collies, 126–27
    Belgian Sheepdogs, 128–29
    Boxers, 130–31
    Brittany Spaniels, 132–33
    Flat-Coated Retrievers, 134–35
    German Shorthaired Pointers, 136–37
    Petit Basset Griffon Vendeens, 138–39
    Siberian Huskies, 140–41
    Staffordshire Bull Terriers, 142–43
    Vizslas, 144–45
Hip dysplasia (HD), 24–25
Holidays, 11
Hounds, *see* Scent hounds; Sighthounds
Housebreaking, 44, 52, 170
Howlers, 51
Huskies, *see* Siberian Huskies
Hygromas, 85
Hypoglycemia, 14

Independence, 42, 50
Indoor companions, 169–86
    Chihuahuas, 172–73
    Italian Greyhounds, 174–75

Japanese Chins, 176–77
Maltese, 178–79
Miniature Dachshunds, 180–81
Papillons, 182–83
Yorkshire Terriers, 171, 184–85
Intelligence, 52
Internet, 16–17, 22, 245–46
Irish Setters, 23, 25, 41
    as not-for-everyone dogs, 234, 239
Irish Wolfhounds:
    as nine-to-five dogs, 92–93
    as sighthounds, 23, 45–46, 92–93, 122
Irrepressible Toy Dog, The (Arden), 243
Italian Greyhounds, 26, 168
    as indoor companions, 174–75

Jack Russell Terriers, 1, 26
    as not-for-everyone dogs, 239–40
Japanese Chins, 102, 168
    as indoor companions, 176–77
Johnson, Lyndon B., 67

Kalina, Shari, 34
Keeshonds, 168, 232
    as family dogs, 112–13
Kinder, Suzanne, 241
Komondors, 42–43
Kuvases, 42–43

Labrador Retrievers, 2, 17, 23–25, 37–39, 122,
    212, 219, 232
    as hard-to-find dogs, 78–79
Lady and the Tramp, 65
Lassie, 108
Leg breaks, 170
Legg-Calves Perthes disease (LCPD), 25
Leg lifting, 170
Lhasa Apsos:
    as non-sporting/rare breed, 25, 54, 234, 240
    as not-for-everyone dogs, 234, 240
Lifestyles, 9
Longhaired Dachshunds, 156, 181
Loudness, 36–37, 42
Love, 5–6
Lowell, Michele, 243
Low-shed breeds, 187–210

Airedales, 188–89
Australian Terriers, 190–91
Bichon Frises, 192–93
Bouvier des Flandres, 194–95
Cairn Terriers, 196–97
Chinese Cresteds, 198–99
Miniature Schnauzers, 200–201
Portuguese Water Dogs, 202–3
Soft-Coated Wheaten Terriers, 204–5
Standard Schnauzers, 206–7
West Highland White Terriers, 208–9

Magazines, 16, 22, 245
Malamutes, *see* Alaskan Malamutes
Males, 12
Maltese:
    as indoor companions, 178–79
    as toys, 26, 51–53, 59, 82, 168, 178–79, 210,
    232
Merle, 58–59
Miniature Dachshunds, 156, 168, 232
    as indoor companions, 180–81
Miniature Pinschers, 13, 25, 168, 186
    as watchdogs, 216–17
Miniature Poodles, 210
    as hard-to-find dogs, 80–81
Miniature Schnauzers, 82, 168, 232
    as low-shed breed, 200–201
Money and expenses, 8
Movement-stimulated nipping, 53
Moyer, Michael, 22
Mutts: America's Dogs (Kilcommons and
    Capuzzo), 34, 244

Nasal-related deafness, 44
Neglect, 3
Neutering, 12, 48
Newfoundland Club of America, 115
Newfoundlands:
    as draft/rescue dogs, 14, 24, 49–50, 114–15, 146
    as family dogs, 114–15
Nine-to-five dogs, 83–102
    Borzois, 84–85
    English Cocker Spaniels, 86–87
    French Bulldogs, 88–89
    Greyhounds, 90–91

Irish Wolfhounds, 92–93
Pekingese, 94–95
Pugs, 96–97
Shih Tzus, 98–99
Whippets, 100–101
Nipping, movement-stimulated, 53
Nonsporting/rare breeds, 54–55
    Chinese Shar Peis, 54, 234, 236–38
    Chow Chows, 54, 234, 238
    Dalmatians, 1, 54, 103, 234, 238–39
    Lhasa Apsos, 25, 54, 234, 240
Norfolk Terriers, 35–37, 122, 208, 210, 232
    as city dogs, 158–59
Norwegian Elkhounds, 28, 146
    as watchdogs, 218–19
Norwich Terriers, 35–37, 122, 208, 210, 232
    as city dogs, 158–59
Not-for-everyone dogs, 233–42
    Akitas, 234
    American Pit Bull Terriers, 234–35
    Australian Shepherds, 235–36
    Basenjis, 236
    Bloodhounds, 236
    Border Collies, 237
    Bulldogs, 234, 237
    Chinese Shar Peis, 234, 236–38
    Chow Chows, 234, 238
    Dalmatians, 234, 238–39
    German Shepherd Dogs, 234, 242
    Irish Setters, 234, 239
    Jack Russell Terriers, 239–40
    Lhasa Apsos, 234, 240
    Old English Sheepdogs, 234, 240
    Rottweilers, 240–41
    Saint Bernards, 234, 241
    Weimaraners, 241–42
Nutrition, 59

Old English Sheepdogs, 24–25
    as not-for-everyone dogs, 234, 240
Older dogs, 12–13
Orality, 38
Owner-sensitivity, 41

Padgett, George A., 237, 243
Palika, Liz, 34

Papillons:
    as indoor companions, 182–83
    as toys, 24, 26, 51–53, 168, 182–83, 232
Pedigrees, 18
Pekingese, 168, 186
    as nine-to-five dogs, 94–95
Pembroke Welsh Corgis, 122, 154
    as watchdogs, 220–21
Petit Basset Griffon Vendeens, 232
    as high-input, high-output dogs, 138–39
Pet stores, 29–30
Pet therapy (pet visitation), 99
Pinschers:
    Doberman Pinschers, 23, 26–27, 46–49,
        68–69, 146, 232, 234
    Miniature Pinschers, 13, 25, 168, 186, 216–17
Pit Bull Terriers, American, 234–35
Pocket Beagles, 67
Pointers, 40–41
    Brittany Spaniels, 27, 40–41, 122, 132–33
    German Shorthaired Pointers, 9, 40–41,
        136–37, 232
    Vizslas, 25, 40–41, 144–45, 232
    Weimaraners, 9, 40–41, 241–42
Pomeranians, 26, 82, 168, 186
    as watchdogs, 222–23
Poodle Club of America, 119
Poodles, 23–27, 55, 232, 234
    Miniature Poodles, 80–81, 210
    Standard Poodles, 23, 82, 103, 118–19, 210
    Teacup Poodles, 81
    Toy Poodles, 80–81, 186, 210
Portuguese Water Dogs, 25, 122, 146, 232
    as low-shed breed, 202–3
Power, 42–43, 48–49
Predatory behavior, 36, 51
Progressive retinal atrophy (PRA), 25
Property guards, 46–49
    Boxers, 23, 46–49, 82, 130–31, 232
    Doberman Pinschers, 23, 26–27, 46–49,
        68–69, 146, 232, 234
    Giant Schnauzers, 46–49
    Great Danes, 13–14, 23, 26–28, 46–49, 76–77,
        102, 232
    Rottweilers, 1, 17, 23, 28, 46–49, 240–41
    see also Flock guards; Watchdogs

Protection, dogs for, 4–5
Protection training, 69
Pugs:
  as nine-to-five dogs, 96–97
  as toys, 24, 51–53, 96–97, 122, 168, 186
Puppies:
  babies with, 11–12
  parents of, 30–31
  see also dogs
Puppy Personality Profile (Volhard and Volhard),
  32
Puppy Report, The (Shook), 244

Rare breeds, see Non-sporting/rare breeds
Rescue dogs, see Draft/rescue dogs
Rescue groups, 17, 19, 28–29
Resources, 243–44
  on breeds, 15–17
Retrievers, 37–39
  Chesapeake Bay Retrievers, 23, 37–39, 146,
    212–13, 234
  Flat-Coated Retrievers, 23, 122, 134–35
  Golden Retrievers, 19, 23–25, 25, 37–39, 58,
    73–74, 122, 235
  Labrador Retrievers, 2, 17, 23–25, 37–39,
    78–79, 122, 212, 219, 232
Rhodesian Ridgebacks, 146, 242
  as watchdogs, 224–25
Roger Caras Dog Book: A Complete Guide to
  Every AKC Breed, The (Caras), 243
Rottweilers:
  as not-for-everyone dogs, 240–41
  as property guards, 1, 17, 23, 28, 46–49,
    240–41
Rubenstein, Eliza, 34
Running-related deafness, 45

Saint Bernards:
  as draft/rescue dogs, 9, 25, 49–50, 234, 241
  as not-for-everyone dogs, 234, 241
Samoyeds:
  as family dogs, 116–17
  as sled dogs, 16, 25, 50–51, 116–17, 232
Save That Dog! (Palika), 34
Scent hounds, 43–45
  Basset Hounds, 43–45, 82, 148–49

Beagles, 23–25, 43–45, 66–67, 219, 232
  Bloodhounds, 43–45, 236
Scenting ability, 43–44
Schipperkes, 146
  as watchdogs, 226–27
Schnauzers:
  Giant Schnauzers, 46–49
  Miniature Schnauzers, 82, 168, 200–201, 232
  Standard Schnauzers, 146, 206–7, 232, 242
Scottish Terriers, 232
  as city dogs, 160–61
Seasons, 10–11
Sebaceous adenitis (SA), 25
Self-confidence, 47
Sensitivity, 46
  to owners, 41
  to sound, 38
  to touch, 37–38
Setters, 41
  English Setters, 41, 110–11
  Gordon Setters, 41
  Irish Setters, 23, 25, 41, 234, 239
Shar Peis, see Chinese Shar Peis
Shedding, 59
  see also Low-shed breeds
Sheepdogs:
  Belgian Sheepdogs, 24, 128–29, 232, 242
  Old English Sheepdogs, 24–25, 234, 240
  Shetland Sheepdogs, 24–26, 47, 53–54, 82,
    122, 228–29
Shelters, 29
Shepherds:
  Australian Shepherds, 12, 23–24, 53–54, 58,
    146, 235–36
  German Shepherd Dogs, 13, 23–25, 28,
    53–54, 58, 72–73, 232, 234, 242
  see also Herding dogs
Shetland Sheepdogs:
  as herding dogs, 24–26, 47, 53–54, 82, 122,
    228–29
  as watchdogs, 228–29
Shiba Inus, 25, 146
  as city dogs, 162–63
Shih Tzus, 24, 26, 82, 168, 186
  as nine-to-five dogs, 98–99
Shook, Larry, 244

Show, breeding for, 38
Siberian Huskies:
    as high-input, high-output dogs, 140–41
    as sled dogs, 23, 25, 50–51, 140–41, 242
Siegal, Mordecai, 245
Sighthounds:
    Afghans, 45–46
    Borzois, 45–46, 84–85
    Greyhounds, 26, 45–46, 90–91, 122, 168,
        174–75
    Irish Wolfhounds, 23, 45–46, 92–93, 122
    Whippets, 2, 9, 45–46, 100–101, 122, 168
Silky Terriers, 168, 186
    as watchdogs, 230–31
Single-family dogs, 43
Single-mindedness, 40
Sizes, 13–14
Sled dogs, 50–51
    Alaskan Malamutes, 2, 9, 50–51, 124–25, 242
    Samoyeds, 16, 25, 50–51, 116–17, 232
    Siberian Huskies, 23, 25, 50–51, 140–41, 242
Small breeds, 14
Smooth Dachshunds, 156
Soft-Coated Wheaten Terriers, 25, 146, 232
    as low-shed breed, 204–5
Sound insensitivity, 38
Space, 9
Spaniels, 39–41
    American Cocker Spaniels, 23–25, 39–40,
        64–65, 76, 120, 168, 234
    Brittany Spaniels, 27, 40–41, 122, 132–33
    Cavalier King Charles Spaniels, 23, 77, 102,
        106–7, 168
    English Cocker Spaniels, 39–40, 76, 86–87,
        122, 168
    English Springer Spaniels, 24–25, 28, 39–40,
        70–71, 146
    Welsh Springer Spaniels, 24–25, 28, 39–40,
        120–21, 146
Spoiling, 52
Staffordshire Bull Terriers, 17, 23, 232, 235, 242
    as high-input, high-output dogs, 142–43
Standard Dachshunds, 232
    as city dogs, 156–57
Standard Poodles, 23, 82, 210
    as family dogs, 103, 118–19

Standard Schnauzers, 146, 232, 242
    as low-shed breed, 206–7
Strong-mindedness, 47
Subluxating patellas, 19–20, 26

Tails from the Barkside (Kilcommons and
        Wilson), 245
Taking action into their own hands, 48
Talkers, 51
Teacup Poodles, 81
Temperament, 47
    testing of, 33
Terriers, 35–37
    American Pit Bull Terriers, 234–35
    Australian Terriers, 168, 190–91, 208, 230, 232
    Border Terriers, 208
    Boston Terriers, 76, 150–51, 186, 232
    Cairn Terriers, 25, 35–37, 168, 196–97, 208,
        232
    Jack Russell Terriers, 1, 26, 239–40
    Norfolk Terriers, 35–37, 122, 158–59, 208, 210,
        232
    Norwich Terriers, 35–37, 122, 158–59, 208,
        210, 232
    Scottish Terriers, 160–61, 232
    Silky Terriers, 168, 186, 230–31
    Soft-Coated Wheaten Terriers, 25, 146, 204–5,
        232
    Staffordshire Bull Terriers, 17, 23, 142–43, 232,
        235, 242
    Tibetan Terriers, 25, 146, 164–65, 210, 232
    Welsh Terriers, 146, 166–67, 210, 232
    West Highland White Terriers, 25, 35–37, 168,
        208–9, 232, 234
    Yorkshire Terriers, 19–20, 26, 51–53, 82, 168,
        171, 184–85, 210, 230, 232, 234
Territorial aggression, 44–45
Therapy Dogs Inc., 99
Therapy Dogs International, 99
Tibetan Terriers, 25, 146, 210, 232
    as city dogs, 164–65
Time, need for, 8–9
Touch sensitivity, 37–38
Toughness, 37, 40
Toy Poodles, 186, 210
    as hard-to-find dogs, 80–81

Toys, 51–53
    Maltese, 26, 51–53, 59, 82, 168, 178–79, 210, 232
    Papillons, 24, 26, 51–53, 168, 182–83, 232
    Pugs, 24, 51–53, 96–97, 122, 168, 186
    training for, 173
    Yorkshire Terriers, 19–20, 26, 51–53, 82, 168, 171, 184–85, 210, 230, 232, 234
Trainers and training, 17–18, 32, 49, 54, 59–60
    classes for, 122
    in crates, 149
    protection, 69
    for toys, 173

UCDavis Book of Dogs: A Complete Medical Reference Guide for Dogs and Puppies (Siegal and Barlough), 245
Understanding Puppy Testing (Clothier), 32, 244
United Kennel Club, 246
Unwanted activity, 53

Vacations, 11
Veterinarians, 17–18, 22, 32
Videos, 16–17, 246
Visually stimulated behavior, 43
Vizslas:
    as high-input, high-output dogs, 144–45
    as pointers, 25, 40–41, 144–45, 232
Volhard, Jack and Wendy, 32, 211
Von Willebrand's disease (VWD), 26

Wandering behavior, 42
Watchdogs, 211–32
    Chesapeake Bay Retrievers, 212–13
    Great Pyrenees, 214–15
    Miniature Pinschers, 216–17
    Norwegian Elkhounds, 218–19
    Pembroke Welsh Corgis, 220–21
    Pomeranians, 222–23
    Rhodesian Ridgebacks, 224–25
    Schipperkes, 226–27
    Shetland Sheepdogs, 228–29
    Silky Terriers, 230–31
    see also Flock guards; Property guards
Weather, and Toys, 170
Weight standards, 58
Weimaraners:
    as not-for-everyone dogs, 241–42
    as pointers, 9, 40–41, 241–42
Welsh Springer Spaniels, 24–25, 28, 39–40, 146
    as family dogs, 120–21
Welsh Terriers, 146, 210, 232
    as city dogs, 166–67
West Highland White Terrier Club of America, 209
West Highland White Terriers, 25, 35–37, 168, 232, 234
    as low-shed breeds, 208–9
Whippets:
    as nine-to-five dogs, 100–101
    as sighthounds, 2, 9, 45–46, 100–101, 122, 168
Wirehaired Dachshunds, 156
Wizard of Oz, The, 196
Wolf hybrids, 51, 234

Yorkshire Terriers:
    as indoor companions, 171, 184–85
    as toys, 19–20, 26, 51–53, 82, 168, 171, 184–85, 210, 230, 232, 234
Younger dogs, 12
Your Purebred Puppy: A Buyer's Guide (Lowell), 243